THE GOOD TEACHER MENTOR

Setting the Standard for
Support and Success

THE GOOD TEACHER MENTOR
Setting the Standard for Support and Success

Sidney Trubowitz
Maureen Picard Robins

Foreword by Seymour B. Sarason

Teachers College, Columbia University
New York and London

Published by Teachers College Press, 1234 Amsterdam Avenue, New York, NY 10027

Library of Congress Cataloging-in-Publication Data

Trubowitz, Sidney.
  The good teacher mentor: setting the standard for support and success / Sidney
  Trubowitz and Maureen Picard Robins; foreword by Seymour Sarason.
    p. cm.
  Includes bibliographical references and index.
  ISBN 0-8077-4387-9 (pbk.)—ISBN 0-8077-4388-7 (cloth)
    1. Mentoring in education—United States. 2. Teachers—Training of—United States. I
Robins, Maureen Picard. II. Title.

LB1731.4T78 2003
370'. 71'5—dc21   2003054022

ISBN 0-8077-4387-9 (paper)
ISBN 0-8077-4388-7 (cloth)

Printed on acid-free paper

Manufactured in the United States of America

10 09 08 07 06 05 04 03   8 7 6 5 4 3 2 1

To my family and Sid, who became family.
—Maureen

*With gratitude to my wife, Naomi, for her invaluable editing help, her
perceptive suggestions and, most of all, her constant support and
encouragement.*
—Sid

Contents

Foreword by Seymour B. Sarason   ix
Introduction   1

Chapter 1 Starting the Mentorship   7
Chapter 2 First Sessions, First Reactions   20
Chapter 3 In the Classroom: Trying Methods from a Book   33
Chapter 4 The Lesson That Fails   49
Chapter 5 Integrating the Academic with the Personal   57
Chapter 6 Other Teachers, Administrators, and the School's Social
   System   62
Chapter 7 Job Pressures   71
Chapter 8 Relating to Parents   77
Chapter 9 The Standardized Test   88
Chapter 10 The End of the Year   95
Chapter 11 What We've Learned   103

Appendix A Sid's Checklist for Mentors   115
Appendix B Maureen's List of Do's and Don'ts for Mentors   117
Appendix C Maureen's List of Do's and Don'ts for Mentees   119

References   121
Suggested Readings   123
Index   129
About the Authors   134

Foreword

Why did it take so long for school systems to take the obvious seriously? The beginning teacher is plagued by doubts, anxiety, questions, unwanted aloneness, lack of collegiality, and fearful of making mistakes that would be judged by others as incompetence, insecure about how to handle problems of discipline, wanting to appear secure at the same time she knows she is putting on an act, and catapulted into a classroom where she is leader and manager for which her academic courses and practice teaching were obviously inadequate.

I have long regarded this state of affairs as morally and professionally scandalous. That is why I regard this book as a major contribution, which should be read by anyone who is part of a teacher preparatory program and by school administrators. I congratulate the authors for their courage, for their candor in revealing their experience as mentor and mentee and what it tells us about the culture of schools and their problem-producing practices.

If, as I believe, not everyone who wants to be a teacher should be allowed to be one, I also believe that not everyone who wants to be a mentor should be allowed to be one. The mentor-mentee relationship should not be one in which one person tells another what to do, period. The mentor does not have a pedagogical cookbook from which he or she can cull a recipe appropriate to a mentee's problem. The mentee is not one who needs a recipe. She has gotten loads of recipes in a preparatory program and in practice teaching where she did little teaching but much recipe following. Above all, the mentee needs to feel safe in a relationship where she can give expression to the thoughts and feelings which destabilize her and have caused her to feel incompetent. The mentee does not need the rhetoric of empty assurance. The mentee needs reassurance that the mentor does not regard her as a whiner, complainer, overly dependent, or worst of all, stupid. The mentee has to feel the mentor truly is trying to understand her in her struggles.

I have known Sid Trubowitz for many years from when I was a participant in an educational reform effort at Queens College. He is, just as Maureen Robins describes him, a listener always sensitive to the feelings of students, teachers, and parents. He knows what he knows but he never

flaunts it. Frankly, if mentoring becomes more widespread but without concern or clarity for selecting mentors, it will be another example of a needed
educational practice gone astray. At the very least, I would hope that those
who select mentors will read this important book, which reads like a novel.

Seymour B. Sarason

Introduction

An urgent dispatch surges through cyberspace to an educator-and-writer listserv, an on-line virtual community. James, a first-year teacher from California, e-mails: "I need some help. This is my first job as a professional teacher. Right now I feel so tired emotionally. Most days are good, but the environment where I work has so many challenges that I feel overwhelmed and [believe] that I am not doing a very good job in service of my students but merely 'the best I can.' How do you keep from allowing all the negative things from beating you? How do you feel that you are making a difference? How do you resist the urge to just have them fill out worksheets or pop in a video out of sheer frustration? How do you get them to simply turn in homework on time and work that is done with some measure of pride? I know this sounds somewhat bleak, but I am feeling burned out at the moment and could use some advice."

These are some of the looming, weighty questions that pour from a first-year teacher's soul. These are the wonderings that emerge so fitfully during a teacher's first year and remain an entire career, still demanding answers.

James doesn't know that yet. Right now he needs to vent his feelings, to cry on someone's shoulder, to be reassured, and to be validated. James needs to know someone, somewhere, is really listening.

Members of his virtual community did what they could to try to rescue James, to repair his teaching self, to salve his wounded self-esteem with messages of acknowledgment, understanding, and advice. A veteran teacher from Texas wrote back. Her response featured the same sharp-eyed assessment and counsel as Dear Abby might have if she had specialized in educational matters. She wrote: "You are suffering from a common feeling among teachers, especially young ones. Here's what you need to do: First, find a colleague you can commiserate with on a regular basis, one in your school who teaches some of the same struggling kids that you do. Stay away from teachers who see the students as lost causes; find a teacher who has the same desire to make a difference as you do."

Her message is a strong one. Find a buddy. Or better, connect with a kindred spirit. Get a mentor.

Mentoring as a means of training and retaining teachers has been part of the educational scene since the early 1980s. It is only recently that policy makers and educational leaders, facing what appears to be a chronic teacher shortage and an attrition rate of almost 30 percent of all beginners, have come to realize the importance of on-site support for neophytes during their first year of teaching. Currently, more than 30 states mandate some form of mentored support for its beginning teachers and other municipalities plan to follow. Urban school systems like that of New York City are working with legislators to ease licensing requirements for mid-career professionals who wish to enter teaching—by relying significantly on mentoring to fill the experience gap.

On-site mentoring could play an even more significant role in the most disadvantaged districts where teacher turnover rates are the highest and the least support is offered.

In systems where seniority determines assignment, often the youngest and least experienced are matched with the most challenging classes or placed in the classes no one else wants. If a first-year teacher lands a challenging assignment but is "certified"—has done student teaching— often this means she is not eligible to participate in a mentoring program. "As a first time teacher *and* one thrown into a junior high inclusion program with severe behavior problems," says Lisa from Virginia, "I was *not* given a mentor because I had supposedly done student teaching (which was mostly student observation and a handful of actual teaching). I felt inadequate and underequipped to deal [with it] properly and was overwhelmed with four classes, homeroom, and extended hours of paperwork. Won't somebody see the light and assist new teachers in a way that could be consistently beneficial toward an earlier degree of success, rather than years of anguish, decreased health, and trial and error?"

Some instructional leaders have heard Lisa's request for help. Not only do mentors guide and orient new teachers, but they also help to keep them in the profession. The Annenberg Foundation created the New Educators Support Team to assist teachers who have been teaching for 1–5 years. But data—and demand from licensed and unlicensed teachers like Lisa—have stimulated the drive to institutionalize mentoring in our school systems. The data suggest that beginning teachers who have access to intensive mentoring by expert colleagues are less likely to leave teaching in the early years. New York State, which now requires a year of mentoring only for uncertified teachers, will broaden the policy in 2004 to include all first-year teachers. And the Board of Education as well as the teachers union would like to expand the mentoring program to 2 years since "most spend a disproportionate amount of time on discipline the first year and do not focus on learning to teach until the second" (Goodnough, 2002, p. 9). Because of viable mentoring programs, three cities in Ohio—Cincinnati, Columbus, and Toledo—and Rochester, New York, have reduced teacher attrition rates by more than two-thirds, often from levels exceeding 20 percent to rates of only 5 percent (Darling-Hammond, 2000).

But what makes mentoring successful? James's virtual mentor from Texas suggested that he find himself a kindred spirit. Could his home state of California do more for James by pairing him arbitrarily with a seasoned teacher? James needs someone he can interact with on a regular basis, someone to show him the ropes, clue him in on the politics of the building, someone to whom he can confess his worry as well as share celebration. Can the special personal qualities of mentoring be transferred to those working in large-scale programs?

Mary, a second-year teacher from Virginia has her doubts:

> Fairfax County, where I teach, does have a mentoring program. It is a great idea in theory but in practice completely depends on whether the mentor and mentee are a good match. My mentor was worthless as a support system. She basically supplied me with a lot of worksheets. She wasn't someone I felt I could go to if I were having a crisis, which I was having essentially the entire year.

"Most of...us are aided by the contact, at strategic points in our life, with people who themselves embody such virtues, such as a sense of what to do and what not to do, even when temptation yanks one sharply in a certain direction," writes Howard Gardener in *Disciplined Minds* (1999). He continues:

> Such a mentoring role has been assumed in the recent past by scientists like Niels Bohr, musicians like Pablo Casals, political leaders like Mohandas Gandhi and Nelson Mandela, writers like Rachel Carson and George Orwell. We need to help young professionals-in-training have personal relationships with (or, at the very least, regular exposure to) such "orienting figures." (p. 250)

We wanted to write a book that examines how professionals-in-training grow with "regular exposure" to an "orienting figure." And what a good time it is to explore ways to help new teachers become acclimated to their careers. About half of all teachers currently in classrooms have taught 5 years or fewer. The U.S. Department of Education predicts schools will need to hire 2 million new teachers this decade alone. Those who teach mathematics, science, special education, or bilingual education are the most prized, as are teachers who agree to work in California, Florida, or Texas, where enrollments are soaring. As many teachers reach retirement age, many new teachers will have to be recruited.

We also wanted to write the kind of book that teachers of retirement status would want to read and be inspired to become mentors. We want others to follow the path of Lynn Skolnik, who for 7 years ran a mentoring program for teachers in Kiamisha Lake, New York. Her program included observations, conferences, and planned lessons she modeled. The group videotaped teachers in action and watched them in pairs or groups. She did a piece on conducting parent conferences and allowed time to discuss "crises and other unplanned events." She says, "I did over 700 classroom observations. I learned so much. I was able to share from one teacher to another. It was a wonderful program." She is currently proposing a mentoring program for mentors in her county.

We wanted to look at the experience of new teachers and what their needs are; we wanted to look at the retiring teachers and explore how they could pass on their valuable experience by becoming mentors and remaining within the educational community.

If mentorships are to prove effective, however, there is a need to understand better what is involved in creating a mentor-mentee relationship that provides growth and satisfaction for both. Simply bringing two adults together is no guarantee of success.

Why This Book?

Required mentoring seems at first to be an oxymoron. While it takes place within a professional context, mentoring is personal. We wanted our book to be personal in terms of the experiences we share, what we reveal to readers and to each other in a language that is vivid and accessible. Many mentoring books lay out a blueprint for the process in dry, clinical language, in a way that suggests the idea of relationship is impersonal, boilerplated, regulated. We aimed to "uncover" rather than cover the topic to reveal the inside story of a first-year teacher and her mentor—her "orienting figure." Our behind-the-scenes look at mentoring lays bare the actions of both partners and how mentoring affects them, as well as showing the development of a teacher. We hope what we offer is both personal and instructive.

The story, told in two voices, offers the perspectives of both mentor and mentee. Its basic narrative arc consists of two people exploring the demands of the educational community and all its varying components— instructional matters, students, colleagues, administrators, and parents. But this arc's understory is equally important: How do the two people in this intergenerational relationship develop trust and deepen their connection to each other while working on a common goal—undertaking a study of the best practices of teaching.

Other books lay out formulas for mentors and offer ideas for new teachers that may or may not work. They are prescriptive, removed from the day-to-day operation of schools, and emanate from higher authority. They see the teacher as receiver of information and knowledge rather than as participant in a process of professional growth. Vera John-Steiner (2000) expresses our view on mentoring best:

> In universities, some of the closest bonds are between professors and doctoral students. In this relationship, we experience the temporary inequality between expert and novice. In time, the relationship changes. The mentor learns new ideas and approaches from his apprentice; he adds to what he learns and transforms it. As the relationship matures, the younger and older participants build a more equal connection. But the journey is not always easy. (pp. 163–164)

The purpose of this book is twofold: to encourage experienced teachers to take on mentorship roles and to lend support and build confidence in the new teacher. We hope that our audience will be intergenerational and we seek to provoke dialogue between seasoned educators and newcomers to the profession. By focusing on how we worked together, we aim to encourage the establishment of positive professional relationships and to demonstrate how new teachers can interact with their colleagues, parents, and the community.

We aim, through this report of our experience, to motivate thinking among those who mentor about ways to help newcomers to the profession make a successful transition into the classrooms and the culture of schools. We also hope that this book will encourage experienced teachers to take on mentorship roles and to consider how professional development can be linked with school improvement efforts by sharing what they learn with colleagues. By focusing on how we worked together we seek to bring about the establishment of positive professional relationships and to demonstrate how new teachers can interact with their colleagues, parents, and the community.

No written material can fully communicate what is involved in helping a newcomer to master the skills needed to work effectively with youngsters. But we have sought, by describing the day-to-day flow of events, to have the reader accompany us on the road to professional development, to experience the obstacles, the satisfactions, the frustrations, and the sense of fulfillment that are all a part of becoming a teacher.

Organization of the Book

This book is organized chronologically over the time we worked together. As we progress through the year we examine a variety of topics ranging from how to conduct a discussion group to the best ways to make use of parent/teacher relationships. In alternating perspectives we discuss our purposes and goals, share our reactions to weekly meetings, in-school interactions, and classroom observations—which often do not go as planned. The book traces our obligations and concerns, and moves through our experience at a middle school in Queens (in New York City) where hallways resonate with the noise of students and their adolescent concerns.

In our first chapter, we share our initial reluctance about entering a mentoring relationship. A shared willingness to experiment and explore what it might be all about prevails. In Chapter 2 Maureen acquaints Sid with her school, and Sid contemplates his role as mentor. In Chapter 3 we begin our work in the classroom and debate the merits of observation. Chapter 4 describes how Sid witnesses a lesson that fails and tries to support Maureen through the experience, and Chapter 5 reports on an observation that turns unpredictable as the class discussion veers off the academic to the personal. Chapter 6 explores the school community and Maureen's role in it, and Chapter 7 discusses job pressures: Maureen frets over her job insecurity and upcoming formal observations and Sid clues her in to how she might cope with these anxieties. In Chapter 8, facing another round of parent-teacher conferences, Maureen asks Sid for his advice on how to do them better. Standardized tests take center stage in Chapter 9. At the conclusion of the year, Chapter 10, Sid and Maureen respond to the need for a different kind of energy and planning. We conclude, in Chapter 11, with what we've learned throughout the year working together.

CHAPTER 1

Starting the Mentorship

Maureen: "Orphan Train Rider"

This was a year of firsts for me. For the first time in my life I had purpose in my career. I had come to do something, to change my life and to involve myself in a professional pursuit where I thought I could make a difference. In my first moments as a teacher I could feel only the awkwardness associated with the first day of school: the stiffness of a new wrinkle-free outfit, new shoes pinching my toes. Because I was hired just 2 days before the opening of school, I hadn't had much chance to familiarize myself with my classroom. The morning before my students entered the room, I was still scanning through files left by my predecessor. I was still opening desk drawers and staring at old, forgotten photos of the staff. I was still browsing through the bookshelves that seemed to map not just the units of study and lesson plans of my predecessor, but the logic of her organization and her interests. As I looked, I tried to imagine my predecessor's teaching life, searching for clues as to what my life here would be.

This is my first experience in charge of a large group of adolescents and I feel a rush of inadequacy. I wonder if I can stay the course, whether I have the stamina. The students file in and sit in any empty seat. I face them unable to decipher what lay behind their expressions. I cannot assess them quickly or thoroughly. I can tell, for example, that the boy in the corner flashing me a smile means something other than that he is happy to be here, but I don't know what. I notice a quiet girl in the corner, but I can't see how manipulative she can be to her classmates outside school. I know nothing of the children's past. I don't know who has been held over, who has lost a parent over the summer, or who the struggling readers are. I know nothing yet of groupthink.

All of them, however, have a better way of reading me. They peg me instantly for my lack of experience. I don't pass out index cards in the way they are used to. I don't give them a rundown of school rules nor do I ask them to suggest their own rules for our classroom community while I chart them. I don't humiliate them. I don't frighten them. I don't tell them how much homework they will get and I don't put a "Do Now" heading on the board. I don't have a seating plan nor do I chatter on about classroom rituals. Beneath their innocence and fresh scrubbed faces they think: "I've got it made."

I have a goal to create a rich literate classroom and I have an idea or two on how to accomplish this. I envision walls teeming with student work, bulletin boards bloomimg beyond their metal borders, shelves heavy with books that kids would want to read. I do not imagine that my adolescents would never put the word *reading* in the same sentence as the word *pleasure*. I do not know portion and proportion: assigning the right amount of homework, balancing a simpler task with a more challenging one, gauging student interest in a lesson or topic. I grope for the "right" tone of voice, gently asserting limitations and expectations. I am naive.

I am flustered by how to correspond with parents. I have already bungled one attempt at parent communication. One of my eighth graders didn't do her homework, so I gave her a form letter stating that she was unprepared for class. When I mention this to another teacher, she gently reminds me that I should have mailed it home to make sure the parents would get it—though we all know that a wily teenager who doesn't want her parents to know that she hasn't done her homework can just as easily intercept the mail.

"Who was the student?" my colleague asks.

I tell her.

"Make sure," she advises, "that any communication sent home is translated into the parent's native language."

I still was a long way from figuring out how to request notes sent home be returned signed in a timely manner and that the signature on the dotted line was not a forgery. After conversing with my colleague, I recalled the introductory packet shown me by an experienced teacher at Louis Armstrong Intermediate School during my internship. In the first few days of school her assignments were geared to revealing a child's personality and responsibility. She would send a meaningless note home and ask for it to be returned signed. She would then collect them and keep them filed, ready for an instant signature check, a veritable forgery detection device. How long the child took to return them was a responsibility indicator.

As the early days of school progressed, I began to see firsthand the gulf between theory and practice. Methods examined and tested in teacher education classes or in supervised classrooms did not yield the same results in my own classroom. Ask teachers-to-be to write a letter to a partner summarizing a chapter of Russell Freedman's *Eleanor Roosevelt: A Life of Discovery* (1993) and you might get some grumbling, but letters with some summary will appear. Ask a seventh-grade class to do the same assignment, and you'll get a few that read, "Waz Up? Man, that Eleanor was ugly. See you after school." No one batted an eye when the professor asked for an "oral" presentation as part of a project, but don't try that on a group of all-too-sexually-aware adolescents.

Normal day-to-day activities became stress points and exercises in unpredictability. So when my principal unexpectedly called me into his office, I could feel my adrenaline redline. "I just got a memo from personnel," he said. "You have to be mentored."

"All right," I responded, wondering what he was talking about, wondering why I had to do this. True, I was a first-year teacher, but I had had *some* classroom experience. I needed some time to get my feet wet. I had just completed a yearlong internship program at Louis Armstrong Intermediate School (I.S.) 227, a middle school that works in collaboration with Queens College, the City University of New York. Promising graduate students in education were granted a stipend to sample middle school life, observe widely, participate in classrooms, and eventually work intimately with seasoned teachers. Despite the prestige and unique blend of experiences, this program didn't satisfy the 16-week student teaching requirement.

"It is a Board of Education and United Federation of Teachers cosponsored program," my principal went on. "Your first meeting is next Tuesday after school. Personnel will pair you with someone."

They would "pair me with someone," I learned later, because no teacher in my school volunteered for the job. For an established teacher, mentoring means extra work and no extra pay. A teacher would have to leave her classroom for three periods a week, and during one of those periods the mentor teacher would have to plan for and teach my class, modeling a lesson. Her own classes would have to be covered. Coverage, though, is an expense. Another teacher giving up her preparatory period would have to be monetarily compensated. Besides, a volunteer teacher would be nearly impossible to find in our tiny, efficient school. Also, coverage is often more work than not having it at all. The teacher still has to create lesson plans for those missed periods, which a substitute has to execute. Often that translates to lost time, with a lesson inadequately taught. The fragile strand of continuous concentration between the teacher and her students would be broken.

No teacher opted for the program.

"Don't worry," my principal offered. "This shouldn't be a problem." He encouraged me to ask another of the young teachers on our staff about his experience with mentoring.

Walking back to my classroom, I resented hidden requirements attached to acquiring a teaching license. I resented what the regulators accepted as transferable classroom experience. And I found that I wasn't the only one to feel that way: Many first-year teachers are shocked by new, secret demands they hadn't foreseen. During this first year of teaching, I had to complete my course work for my masters in education and take additional Board of Education classes that would total 60 hours of new-teacher training. Why did I need both a master's and new-teacher credits at the same time? And now, on top of this, mentoring. Then there was the matter of why I was here in the first place: to teach. I had to create lessons plans, read books for two seventh-grade and two eighth-grade classes, each with a different program. My first-year teacher requirements seemed never ending. I grew tired just thinking about them.

I fretted about my life and how little of it I would have this year. I began to resent the requirements for a job that paid less than other professionals. But I had a vision, a goal. After years of wandering between career options, I'd found something I really loved. Teaching is not a job; it's a way of life. Of course I would comply with the mentorship requirement.

I began to worry about the mentor I would be paired with. I'm idiosyncratic, I thought. I'm older, not a freshly minted college graduate. I already had a master's degree in my content area. My imagination began to get the better of me. I imagined being paired with Mr. K., my slow-moving, moody, and uninspiring English teacher from the eighth grade. I envisioned long, endlessly tiresome sessions with Mr. K., who would scratch his double chin as if he were actually considering what I was saying—but wasn't—as he did way back then. Or I would be paired with some crackerjack disciplinarian who would coach me in ways of setting limits, behavioral modification, and disciplinary tactics. Or I would be paired with a burned-out veteran who would come by for a minute and say, "I want to do this about as much as you want to do this—not at all."

I realized that I had a dim view of teachers. Did I really think I could be such a different kind of teacher? And if I had these negative views of teachers—particularly those from middle school—what on earth did the kids think?

I decided to try to be open-minded. It would take a while to become that different kind of teacher I imagined for myself.

I took my principal's advice and consulted the other teacher who had experienced the mentoring program.

"It wasn't too bad," he said.

"What actually happened?" I asked.

He told me a retired teacher from our district came to work with him once a week. He came to enjoy her visits. She had given him some good classroom management pointers, he said. "Like asking the student who was talking the most to become a monitor."

That was all right, but it wasn't enough. If I were going to have a mentor, I needed one to teach me how to relate to a couple of angry parents who scheduled a meeting for the next day. I needed to learn how to clock parent meetings at open school night. I needed to know whether or not it was right for me to stop two boys in my homeroom from fighting across the street after school. I needed someone who could help me articulate a vision of a book-loving, literate classroom. I needed someone to continue the training launched with my internship at Louis Armstrong (I.S. 227). There, I was challenged to find my "teaching voice"—to take risks, to visit and observe other teachers, to try out styles and lessons until I could find what was right for me and know why it was right. Would my mentor sustain that quest?

I decided not to wait. I executed a preemptive strike. I phoned one of my professors from Queens College, hoping that he would be able to facilitate a match—or persuade someone to take me on. I had immediately asked for my previous advisor and mentor from Louis Armstrong, Sid Trubowitz. I knew that he was retired but was still active in a variety of teacher education programs.

Would Sid do it?

Then Tuesday rolled around. Sid had not responded, and no other candidate for mentoring appeared. A pot of coffee and a platter of donuts anchored the table around which six pairs of senior and junior teachers were seated. All had been paired by Personnel and had had at least one informal meeting. I was the only unmatched attendee. I looked around and saw that the couples had already bonded. The younger ones were looking adoringly at the veterans, eager to imprint their style, imitate their responses, drink in their experience. When the team leader outlined instructions, I could see the mentors nodding or winking at their mentees. They were already developing their secret language, their code. I noticed one young woman imitating the mannerisms of her mentor. It reminded me of a student teacher/teacher pair I knew at Louis Armstrong. By the end of their weeks together they had grown quite similar—they even dressed alike.

"Have you found a mentor for me?" I asked the meeting coordinator.

"Not yet," she replied.

I felt like the child described so vividly by Andrea Warren in her book (1997), the orphan who put on his Sunday best but, alas, was not selected and returned to the westward train. I went home confused at the depth of my feelings. I was excited suddenly about the possibility of being close to someone, of being able to talk out the issues, the adjustments, and the wonder of the entire experience. I had not been prepared for the sheer intimacy of the teacher-student relationship, the day-to-dayness of it all. How personal an experience it is to convey knowledge, to motivate kids to learn, to work harder, to achieve goals set by you.

I went home high on caffeine and possibility—but without a mentor.

Maureen: A Mentor Is Chosen. What Can I Expect?

Several weeks passed and no word about a mentor. Finally, Sid, who had initial misgivings, decided to come aboard. I was enormously relieved. At least I knew that I would have a mentor whose approach to teacher training was one that I was familiar with. He encouraged teachers to construct their own knowledge about their methods and to find their own teaching voices. I began to jot things down in a notebook for two reasons. First, I wanted to remember all the items I planned to discuss with him, and there was such an onslaught of issues that I needed to use writing as a way to hold onto them. Second, I knew that Sid was a big proponent of reflective practice and of keeping a thoughtful log. I assumed that I would continue keeping a log as I did for him at Louis Armstrong, and he would read it and pencil comments in the margins.

My first entry was short and listlike:

- What professors overlook, forget, or omit teaching in ed school
- Meeting kids for the first time
- Writing good handouts, parent communications
- Hormones—there's a lot of touching going on.

Even though I was looking forward to seeing Sid and the resolution of the problem of "Who Will Be My Mentor?" I was nervous too. There's always anxiety when working with someone closely to the degree that a one-to-one relationship promises. Sid would be observing me, examining the way I conduct myself, the way I relate to kids, the lessons I plan, everything. He would be seeing things about me that I wouldn't know enough to be self-conscious about. I wanted this to be a year of self-deceit. I wanted to put "ignorance is bliss" to work to help me through the year. I wanted to pretend that this wasn't such a difficult job. I wanted to steamroll my way through. I had just been declared able to be on my own, and now I would have a chaperone. This was a big deal to me, unlike practiced, self-confident teachers who were used to having other adults in their rooms whether they were student teachers or visitors or observers. I didn't want a visitor in the room to make me second-guess everything I was doing or not doing. I was not really ready for Sid.

None of these things came into play when Sid arrived. The sight of him comforted me. I recalled his easy manner when we worked together when I was an intern at Louis Armstrong. I recalled the way he listened as the interns poured out their hearts. I remembered how he listened to me describe the growing cognitive dissonance between the theory I was learning in education school and actual classroom practice. Who cared about John Dewey? I just needed to find the light switch to signal students it was time to come together again. Sometimes a simple issue spoken while eating lunch with him and the other interns before our formal meeting would be transformed into an enormous "teachable moment." Sid looked for those moments, when a small issue, an off-the-cuff remark, became a learning experience in between bites of baby carrots.

"Sid," I said and shook his hand.

"Here we are," he said. "Let's go get something to eat and we can talk."

I grabbed my coat and ushered him to the nearest eatery, Wendy's. I did not want him to even enter the building. What I had to say was private. He let me talk for an hour about everything on my mind. I also had my list in my log, started a while back, that had now grown to include items like "what do you say in a meeting of staff evaluators and parents," "what do you do when one child injures or steals or cheats off another child," and "what about that feeling, the first-year feeling, that next year, you are sure of it, you'll be a better teacher." I had just lost my temper with a class for the first time: Was that all right? How do I rebound from that? And how was I going to accomplish all that I had to my first year: establishing relationships, planning lessons, going to graduate school, getting those new-teacher credits, raising a family?

I showed my log list to Sid. He read through it as I gulped down some coffee. I watched him read and scribble. He returned my notebook. After I got back to school, I deciphered his penciled scrawl: "Maureen, at some point in the near future let's take these one at a time."

Sid affirms my assessments even though I'm wobbly and not confident as I speak. He nods or uses his voice to confirm that he is listening, and listening deeply. He takes his own notes to ponder future avenues of discussion, and thinks out loud as to what they might be. During our first meeting he is very much the therapist, encouraging the new client to ramble on. At the close of our meeting we establish the times we would meet, that we would e-mail each other, or phone, and that I would keep a log. I would record my wonderings, observations, and ponderings much as I did as an intern. He would read my log, write comments, and discuss them when he visited. I went home that day feeling unburdened. Lightened. My thinking freed of accumulating worries, I could again return to my overarching goal that began when I was an intern: to find my teaching voice.

As I prepared my lessons for my seventh graders, a connection occurred to me. We were reading Lois Lowry's novel set in a utopian universe, *The Giver* (1993). I immediately connected Sid with The Giver and myself with Jonah, the young apprentice. Sid had history; he had knowledge; he had experience. In the book, The Giver lays his hands on Jonah's back and transmits memories. He begins by offering sweet, pleasant experiences to Jonah. Then the real work begins, and The Giver transmits painful memories of sunburn, a broken bone, war. Jonah loses his innocence and begins to question more deeply, and he sharpens his focus.

If only Sid could transmit memory and experience through the laying on of hands. But he cannot.

Sid: Getting Involved in the Mentorship

It began with a telephone call. Maureen Robins, whom I knew as an intern at I.S. 227 where I had been Director of the Queens College–Louis Armstrong Middle School Collaboration, asked me to work with her to fulfill a New York State requirement that all Preparatory Provisional Teachers (PPTs) receive mentoring. PPTs are newly hired, uncertified teachers, and the aim of the mentorship is to help them acquire effective teaching strategies.

I didn't want to take time from writing and the leisure of retirement, so my first reaction to Maureen's request was "No." I'd been taking a class at the West Side YMCA in memoir writing following up on something I've been wanting to do for years: to capture and record my growing-up experiences and the story of my life as a teacher. I'd had thoughts of learning Italian, and I'd been playing with the idea of taking a course in Montepulciano, a small town in Tuscany where my daughter had studied. I'd also been anticipating the birth of my first grandchild and wanted to be ready to spend a lot of time with her. Did I want to postpone these plans to commit myself to working with Maureen every week for an entire year?

My reluctance to become involved was strengthened when I learned that if I were to participate in the mentorship program, I'd have to get fingerprinted and obtain a per diem teacher's license. I saw warning signs saying "Beware of working in any formalized Board of Education venture. You'll get swallowed up by bureaucratic red tape." I was put off further when I was told that I needed to attend a course for prospective mentors. After 40 years of experience as a public school teacher, principal, college professor, college administrator, and a project director guiding newcomers and veterans alike, I wasn't ready to take a course in how to mentor. I didn't think I needed the Board of Education to define how I should operate as a mentor, to make me over in an image they had in mind.

As I was about to reject the idea of becoming a mentor, a colleague called to urge me to work with Maureen. "You and Maureen can find out what it takes for an experienced educator and a new teacher to work together. You can make a real contribution. Mentoring is going on everywhere. New principals are assigned mentors. Businesses seek mentors for their new employees. Civic groups advertise for mentors for inner-city youngsters. And now the State Department of Education has mandated mentoring for uncertified teachers."

I considered what he said, and the idea that I still had an important contribution to make was appealing. I was also grappling with how to handle free time after job requirements had shaped my week for so many years. I was finding the transition from a clearly defined workweek to unstructured time that I had to organize for myself was not easy. I also didn't want to let go of being a part of schools, of putting aside all that I had learned about education over the years. Serving as a mentor would give me some of the structure I found I needed, and it would keep me involved. The prospect of working once a week with Maureen, whose intelligence and creativity I was familiar with from our days together at the Louis Armstrong Middle School, became more attractive.

I thought back to my own initiation into teaching. I had just received a masters degree in the teaching of English from Teachers College, Columbia University, when armed with a substitute license I entered the Brooklyn High School of Automotive Trades in the Greenpoint section of Brooklyn, the school to which I had been assigned by the New York City Board of Education. The English Department chairman handed me a roll book, told me a room number, and sent me on my way. It was my first time in a high school since my own student days, as practice teaching hadn't been part of my preparation. And now I found myself alone in a bare, empty classroom getting ready to impart knowledge and wisdom to Latinos, African Americans, and a handful of white youngsters who came from backgrounds so different from my own. At 24, I was unsure of who I was, uncertain about whether I wanted to remain a teacher, and uninformed about what it takes to run a classroom of adolescent boys. I struggled through the year attempting to teach Wordsworth, Coleridge, and Longfellow to students interested only in learning the intricacies of auto mechanics. I had no one to talk to, no one to learn from, and no one to guide me though the tumultuous year of first-year teaching. It was a tough and lonely time. I needed someone to lead me past the shoals of self-doubt and inadequacy.

I reconsidered my initial response to Maureen's request. I've spent my professional life guiding new teachers, but I don't think I've ever systematically looked into what it is I do or don't do that contributes to or inhibits teacher growth. I have always known that assisting a new teacher involves more than suggesting ideas or providing material, and that most important of all is the development of a relationship leading to knowledge that is internalized and adds to the new teacher's sense of confidence. That sounds simple enough, but how it will play out is complicated. As Maureen's mentor, someone designated to show her the way to teacher effectiveness, I knew the road ahead involved more than communicating facts and specific techniques. I also recognized that how you help someone grow can't be blueprinted.

As I saw retired personnel, experienced instructors, people everywhere embarking on mentorships trusting only to their instincts and good intentions, the prospect of working with Maureen became even more appealing. We could give others moving into mentorships the perspectives of both mentor and mentee and by doing so provide insights into what it takes to develop a successful relationship. By describing in detail and in depth our ongoing interaction, we could produce material not only of value to others but which would have the additional benefit of focusing us both on what we had to do to make the mentorship work.

Although I have a deep reservoir of experience, I am still awed and humbled by the prospect of leading someone through the trials of first-year teaching. How can I begin to assist someone to deal with the trepidation, the insecurities, the uncertainties, and the gaps in knowledge that are part of learning about a school, the other teachers, the administrators, the parents, and the students? I have no formulas to offer for helping someone to become skilled and fulfilled as a teacher. All I can bring to a mentorship is who I am and what I know. I tell Maureen I am ready to try. And so we begin.

Sid: The Mentor Considers His Goals

The challenge of working to help a person grow as a teacher is formidable, but it's something I've been doing all my professional life. With the start of this new project I feel a growing excitement, and my creative juices begin to flow. Before meeting with Maureen, I list my goals of what a mentorship with Maureen will be:

- To help her gain confidence
- To increase her knowledge of instructional approaches
- To have her become part of the school staff
- To show her ways to work with the bureaucracy
- To give her a sense of achievement
- To have her believe that teaching is a profession worthy of pride

My words seem inadequate for I can't give her what only comes with experience. Ahead of her are moments of discouragement, the making of mistakes, the sense of not having done enough to help children, the times of frustration. I wish I could wave a magic wand and move her painlessly through the trials of beginning teaching. I know this cannot be.

The words of different first-year teachers come to mind. One told me, "I've had only 7 weeks of preparation, and when a parent asks me a question, I feel like a fraud." Another said, "I worried that I'd walk into a classroom, close my door, and the only adult voice I'd hear all day would be my own." I hear others and their persistent questions: "Where do I go for books and paper?" "How do I get my clerical work done?" "What am I supposed to teach?" "How will the principal judge my work?" "Will I be able to control my class?" "Will the children like me?" "What will my colleagues think of me?" As I think of their concerns, I imagine how overwhelming these beginning days of teaching must be.

It is not surprising that within the first weeks of the fall semester there are those who have found the task of leading classes of 30 or more children too hard to handle and leave teaching for less stressful positions.

I think about what I can do as mentor so that Maureen does not join the exodus of first-year teachers leaving the school system. I jot down ideas. They include listening, supporting, encouraging strengths, providing resource materials, asking questions, exchanging ideas, providing perspective on her struggle.

I know that the specifics of what I do are less important than how I do them. I have seen supervisors operate as though teaching is "telling" and responses are not expected. I aim to engage Maureen in conversation rather than to view her as an audience. Our relationship will be both equal and unequal: We will be learning together, and yet there will be times I will clearly be the instructor. I want to be a resource to help Maureen maintain the ideals and dreams she shared with me at Louis Armstrong.

As I read the material about mentorship provided by the district office, I realize that increasingly things in New York City are done by the number. Accountability means filing a set number of observation reports, submitting weekly lesson plans, gauging progress by scores on standardized tests, giving regularly scheduled examinations, and filling out attendance sheets. The Board of Education memorandum on mentorship prescribes demonstration lessons, intervisitations, classroom observations, and postobservation conferences. It mandates that I must teach one period a week and that only recent retirees (retired no more than 3 years) may be selected as mentors. I am permitted to mentor Maureen, even though I don't meet the requirements, because district personnel familiar with work I had done for them on previous occasions, choose to make an exception.

This foretells that this mentorship won't be handled by the book.

I go to I.S. 250 where Maureen is an English teacher, and I am struck by the fact that schools in New York City are most often identified by number rather than by name. I enter the building and approach a security guard seated in a glass-enclosed cubicle to submit to the usual procedure of showing identification, indicating my destination in the building, and signing my name. I have come to a world designed to wall off outside threats.

I am puzzled by the dilemma facing educators in that there is agreement that parent and community involvement is desirable and yet at the same time the need exists for schools to be converted into fortresses guarding against the incursion of outsiders. Nowhere at the entrance to buildings is the sign that reads "Welcome to our school. In order to guide you better, please go to the main office." Rather, there is the threat that prosecution awaits anyone who dares to enter without first reporting to the principal. I wonder how Maureen and other teachers feel as each day they walk past uniformed personnel who are there to shield them from perils lurking outside. The fact is, there are no metal detectors here and it appears to be minimum, rather than maximum, security. Do they begin to equate every unfamiliar adult face with danger? When they read sensational news stories of attacks on teachers, do they become wary of dealing with hostile parents? Is there confusion between the messages "We want you in" and "Keep out"?

I face the reality that mentoring does not occur in a vacuum, that it isn't simply a relationship that develops within the four walls of a classroom, that the outside environment affects what the teacher does with students. I know, for example, that Maureen and I together will have to counter a view held by many schools that parents and the public in general are best kept distant from what goes on in the classroom, since during the year I will be exploring with Maureen how to get parents involved in class activity. I recognize that we will constantly have to deal with other institutional facts of life—such as a rigid time schedule, overcrowded classrooms, and poor physical settings—that stand in the way of good education. Part of my task as mentor is to help her deal with them and to encourage her to work with others to effect positive school change.

On coming into the main hallway I see all kinds of students—tall, short, womanly, childlike, smartly dressed students, youngsters in sweat shirts and baggy pants. On a wall is a sign reminding students of Pajama Day and the need to dress appropriately. What a key word is *appropriate!* Isn't that what adolescents struggle to define for themselves? What clothes will allow me to feel comfortable with my friends and yet acquiesce to the demands of adults? How can I channel inner feelings that sometimes take over my body and mind? How do I show the boy or girl across the room that I like him or her and want to be liked in return?

I think to myself that this is a group that needs so much, demands so much. The teacher's job is large.

CHAPTER 2

First Sessions, First Reactions

Maureen: Exploring the School Environment

Sid's white hair telegraphs his presence as I rush down the hall to greet him at the school's security desk. Immediately, Sid asks me to introduce him to our principal so he's not a "stranger walking in" and to show him around so that he can get a feel for the school. Each school, he often told me when I was a beginning intern, has its own environment, its own culture. It's being "A Walker in the School," I call it, naming it after Alfred Kazin's memoir, *A Walker in the City*, a book Sid and I had often discussed. When I was an intern under his direction at I.S. 227, he advised me to absorb the environment, to linger in the lunchroom, to sit in the gym bleachers and watch basketball practice, to get the smell and the sound of the school, to do whatever I needed to do to feel at home at the school and comfortable in its environs. And now he wants to do the same here.

The tour begins at the entrance. This school is not strictly representative of New York City public schools. Housed within one squat, nondescript building is one of the few successful high school and middle school collaborations, RFK High School and I.S. 250. Staggered schedules between the two schools and a no-bell system are some of the few adaptations that seem to make this collaboration work. Territories are sketched out—leaving both entities feeling cramped. Much of the building is considered high school space, and special events need to be carefully choreographed when involving the cafetorium or the gym.

The two separate educational entities share a philosophy that relationships and cooperation—between students and between students and teachers—take precedence. Service learning is a basic educational building block and is built into all schedules.

Middle school students are chosen through an application process when they are in the fourth grade. It is not a school for the gifted or for those who are in desperate need of remediation. This is an organization for kids who otherwise might "fall between the cracks," as some say. Ideally, the school was created for children who did well on tests but not in class or vice versa. Kids come to this school to be considered as a person rather than a number.

My classroom, too, is not typical as far as New York City public schools go. The seventh and eighth graders in four small classes rotate around "areas" in a large book-lined room that was once a library. The "areas" are defined by furniture and the direction the seats face. If scheduling permits, only three classes operate simultaneously, while a fourth is out of the room—in gym, art, or one of the regulation-sized classrooms occupying the first and second floors of the larger building. Sometimes one class would not meet in the same place two times in a row.

In some ways, the open classroom for the middle school is unworkable and the teachers and principal know it. Children who are easily distracted are often distracted. There is a plan under consideration to take this room and restore it to a library, sectioning off a part of it with a wall to form a classroom for me. The other classes will be given miniature rooms carved out of what now houses the library and office on the second floor. When people talk about this plan, they whisper. The hushed voices teach me something about Board of Education culture: Never believe a plan for school construction until it appears right in front of you.

The concept of being a school without walls happened by accident, I'm told by founding teachers. The school was part of a small-school initiative—"small schools in a big city"—and the incubator space was a large area without walls housed in a functioning elementary school. That was 7 years ago with a school register of 50 children. Now, with 160 boys and girls, the school seems packed to the max. Special regulations limit class size at an intimate 20 pupils. The fifth- and sixth-grade classes are cross-graded, I tell Sid, as we walk down the hall and meet one of the teachers.

"Do you remember me?" she asks Sid coyly. To me she says, "Sid was one of my teachers way back when."

"Of course," Sid responds.

While they catch up on small talk, I consider how many teachers Sid must have trained over the years. I remember the group of interns who studied under him, how he elevated the nature of their thoughts by bringing in all sorts of issues, from newspapers, teacher chat, and educational thinkers. Of course, he had us reflecting in a log, a written account of what we had done that week and what we thought about it.

We were asked to write about the experience of teaching our lessons and wonder on paper whether or not our lessons accomplished what we had intended. We were asked to consider how lesson plans came alive in the classroom. We were to reflect on the differences between a lesson written down on paper and the execution of it in the classroom. We were to "kid watch" and jot down our observations. We were asked to observe each other and write down our impressions. The interns depended on him to organize their thoughts, to confirm their observations, to reinforce their efforts during a weekly postlunch session.

I feel odd without the other interns to hide behind, yet I also feel special to have Sid all to myself.

I explain to Sid, on our way upstairs to the library, that the school is small. I am the only member of the staff who teaches seventh- and eighth-grade English, though there is a full complement of English teachers in the high school. We reach the library. The library, for Sid, as I have learned, is the heart of the school. He peeks in. "It's tiny!" he exclaims in a loud whisper.

"But powerful," I say, responding the way our librarian does when she greets visitors who react similarly.

He wrinkles his nose. For Sid, taking kids to the library is one of the most meaningful ways to create lovers of reading. "This is so different from the Louis Armstrong library," he allows.

It's only natural that we begin to compare I.S. 250 to Louis Armstrong. Why not? There is a vast difference from the Louis Armstrong Middle School where I received most of my training and first met Sid. Louis Armstrong has 1,600 students with a constant influx of Queens College student teachers, interns, and other staffers. I.S. 250 is tiny. Its ambition is to provide personal attention to children who might otherwise fall between the cracks. I.S. 250 shares a building with a high school and is reminded of it constantly when scheduling programs and activities.

We head back downstairs talking about how this building is primarily high school turf. Bulletin boards reflect high schoolers' work and concerns. A board posting a schedule of college recruiters greets most visitors at the entrance. Similarly, the high schoolers get priority over the gym. But the fact that there is a collaboration between high school and middle school tempers the environment. Cohabitation reminds us to be considerate neighbors and so hallways need to be quiet. Yet, this school, like so many other urban facilities, uses every inch of space and sometimes a class will cozy up in a corner of the hall, students seated on the floor, watching an instructional video, reading quietly, or holding a discussion.

We return to my "area." Many teachers might not want to teach in such an environment. Some call it a fishbowl because everything you do or say is visible and audible to everyone.

"How are you relating to the other teachers?" Sid inquires.

"All right," I tell him. "I'm picking up ways they manage their classes." I have been observing three different teachers with three different teaching styles. I note that our social studies teacher likes to teach out of a textbook and never, absolutely never, raises his voice. Our science teacher loves technology and often develops projects for the children to work on in groups using the computer. He's got a wonderful sense of humor, and the children love the way it can defuse a tense situation. And our math teacher is a no-nonsense young woman who has a strong command of her content and excellent classroom management.

Actually, it's not teacher watching—or my relationship with the teachers—that I'd like to talk about. I'm still overflowing with questions and comments about my puzzling, emotional, and draining job. I go home each night and collapse as if I've spent the day doing physical labor, walking a beat, or moving furniture. I want to learn a quick, reliable way to plan my lessons, and be able to read through my book closet the way Bookworm could speed-read in *Batman*—simply by placing a hand over each page of type. I want to know what I'm really seeing when I kid watch. I want to inhale an automatic manner of talking to parents and acquire an internal tone gauge on how to write notes home. And even more, I want to figure out what this whole mentorship thing is really about.

Sid: Weathering a Rush of Questions

This first meeting becomes a time for Maureen to talk about her concerns and they come rapidly:

- I feel so self-critical.
- There's so much to learn.
- I have to learn how to "read" a class. What are they like? The kids are well practiced at reading a teacher.
- What do you do when you're losing your temper?
- What makes a good letter to parents?
- What do you do when kids ignore other kids during advisories?
- How do I manage all the professional development requirements? (mandated new-teacher workshops; finishing courses for my masters)
- How do I deal with all the other people in the school? Other teachers? The custodian? The administration?

I note that these questions refer not to curriculum matters or narrow pedagogical concerns but rather to relationships and to the problems of managing one's life and feelings.

I remind myself to let Maureen talk. These first meetings need to be a time for unbottling all the feelings and ideas that lie unexpressed inside a new teacher. I need to be stingy with interruptions or suggestions and not feel any compulsion to establish myself as a knowledgeable mentor. This is not easy, for I want to feel valued, to be thought of as helpful. But I'm aware that only by allowing her to speak freely will I get a clear picture of her concerns, and take the first steps in establishing a relationship of trust.

But soon the mode of our meetings changes from one in which I listen and Maureen talks to one in which we together explore issues of concerns. Maureen reviews for me something that has been bothering her, what she describes as a major error in communicating with parents. She had given a note to a student for her parent reporting that she hadn't been doing her homework. Questions arise about whether the note will ever reach home or be returned with the parent's signature forged. We discuss the problem.

Maureen tells me that she sent the note home so that the parent would get after the kid to do her homework. I point out that the parent's reaction is likely to be negative, that she'd punish the girl, withdraw a privilege, reprimand her, or do something the youngster wouldn't like to have happen. With that being the case, some kids might do whatever they could to avoid having the parent receive the note—not deliver it, intercept the letter in the mail box, even forge a signature. I urge Maureen to consider why the student is not doing her homework. It may be that her work habits are poor or that the assignment has no meaning for her or that it is her way of showing resistance to the teacher and the school. I suggest that face-to-face conversation is more likely to help than a note sent home.

I think to myself that there is a danger for Maureen, as there is for many new teachers, of falling into a pattern of applying superficial responses to problems, of following the example of what many experienced teachers do to get students to conform: If a student doesn't do his homework, send a note to the parent whose job it becomes to harangue the child into compliance. Too quick, too simple, not likely to deal with the causes of a problem.

Sid: A Mentor Talks to Himself

After these initial interactions with Maureen I pause to consider again what makes for good mentoring. I look back at my own experience.

I grew up in an immigrant family where the focus was on working hard and keeping everyone in good health, a family without much mentoring. There was no one to show me how to tie my shoe laces, no one to run down the street holding on to the back of my bicycle as I tried to stay balanced, no one to take me to baseball games, no one to sit by my side watching television, no one to ask me about school. In high school and college when playing basketball was so central to my life, my coaches were not mentors either since they cared for nothing about me except my ability to play ball. They never asked how my classes were going or inquired about my future plans. They just wanted me to practice in the gymnasium and perform well in games.

But then I think about Bertha Padouk, a reading teacher at P.S. 154, where I started teaching in an elementary school. Bertha spoke with a stereotypical New York accent. She had scraggly hair, brown eyes, and a gentle but firm way with children. I was 25 and in my second year of teaching. She came to my fifth-grade class to help me develop an individualized reading program. In college I had been an English major and I liked books. I didn't know much about the technical aspects of reading—locating the main idea, finding details, teaching comprehension, and so on. But I got excited about literature, and after my fifth graders and I gathered books from the local library and family collections, we had panel discussions, dressed up as book characters, wrote to authors, created dramatizations, and read, read, read.

There was a quiet quality about Bertha. I never felt as though I was being judged. I was given ideas—how to do individual diagnoses, names of good books, what to look for in student conferences. She brought lots of books into the classroom. She'd stay in the class and work with me. Her help was substantial and yet not intrusive. In time, I was asked to talk to teachers in other schools about my approach to reading. I was made to feel special.

In thinking about my growing-up years, I've come to the belief that we all crave mentoring, someone to look up to. We look for models, people we like, people we want to emulate. I think again of Bertha Padouk. She gave me a sense of power, that I could do, that I was doing. She put muscle on my sense of self. Having a mentor is like having a genie in a bottle, someone we can call on to enhance our inner strength.

I don't think we ever outgrow our need for mentoring, for someone who will listen, someone with whom we can share our attempts to live and work well. I want to be for Maureen what Bertha Padouk was for me.

As our initial Wednesday meeting is about to end, Maureen says, "You fall in love with the kids. I never expected the whole thing to be so emotional. I have to learn to make accommodations between my professional and personal life."

Maureen's comments cause me to wonder how a teacher feels both an attachment for her students and at the same time maintains a distance.

Teaching is a tough job in that we struggle to have boundaries, to care deeply about kids and yet not to be so fully absorbed that we neglect our families and other interests.

I consider how to help her find the right balance between home and school, between family demands and professional obligations. Maybe, if, at our meetings we talk about things other than education—movies, books, politics, our children—we will be reminded that teaching calls upon us to be people who involve themselves in many areas.

Concerns arise not only for Maureen but for me as well. I think about the need to deal not only with techniques but also with concepts. I wonder about how to move our talks from discussions of the immediate to considerations of larger issues. I ponder the problem of staying connected even though we see each other only once a week.

I recognize that, with more and more underprepared people being thrust into classrooms as teachers, there will be pressure to give immediate answers to problems, to offer a string of teaching recipes. For me, the goal of the mentorship is to help Maureen figure out her own solutions to difficulty. It is not simply a matter of giving her a script to follow outlining steps to be taken. I understand that specifics have to come in to play and that keeping someone in the profession is a goal. I'm conflicted about approaching the problem of how to help a teacher survive the first year's trials and tribulations. I realize a teacher needs a classroom where routines are ingrained and the day proceeds in an orderly fashion. But I'm also aware that if we look exclusively to survival, we will only perpetuate the status quo.

I look at teaching as so much more than gaining mastery of a set of prescribed skills. It is an art that involves learning a culture, learning about oneself, developing a sensitivity to students and parents, as well as learning instructional techniques. I also believe that the mentor doesn't operate in a mechanical fashion, but sees what may work with one person may not be effective with another. Here, too, it is a matter of understanding the situation, knowing the person, and being aware of your own response. For now, the approach is feeling out for what we want to do, for how we want to proceed, with the hope that through our ongoing conversations about Maureen's experience we will achieve new insights as partners in thought.

We decided it would be useful for each of us to keep a log. I recall how, as Director of the Queens College–Louis Armstrong Middle School Collaboration, the log I maintained helped me clarify my role, see the strengths and weaknesses of what we were doing, and be aware of the tensions that were part of the effort to link college faculty with public school personnel (Trubowitz, 1984, pp. 66–72). Writing about what I experienced and commenting on what happened gave me a sense of control, a sense that

I wasn't a passive spectator to events. I anticipated that my log on mentoring would assist me to do the same. I saw our logs as a way of bringing me into Maureen's classroom regularly even though we wouldn't be meeting each day. Reflecting in writing was a way of staying in the present, of being ever conscious of what was happening as we worked together. I know how easy it is for thoughts to fly through your head and be forgotten if they're not recorded. My log would allow me to capture ideas and feelings that would be lost if they weren't written down. I wanted my log to keep me alert to how the mentorship was progressing, to how I was interacting with Maureen, and to how she was responding. We agreed that we would use our logs to focus on issues that arise in the school as well as those that occur in the classroom. In our comments we would look at ourselves as well as at students, the school faculty, the administration, and the building environment. I started to make log entries and to respond to Maureen's log, which she shared with me.

Maureen: My Log

I think things through by writing them down, and so I am constantly recording my ideas, describing my emotions, and framing questions in a notebook or a laptop whenever I have a moment. Before I leave for school, I review my preparation schedule and who's going to pick up my children at the end of their school day so I can squeeze in time for isolating that day's key incidents and examining my reactions to them. Jotting my thoughts on paper encourages me to reflect and reframe my notions in questions I want to ask Sid.

My log entries so far have mostly consisted of lists. I am beginning to stretch my thoughts out a bit. I'm preoccupied with topics that are gray and soft rather than with the nuts and bolts of teaching content. I need to know how to respond to kids and how to respond naturally in challenging circumstances I've never experienced before. I need to know what to do when a child injures another, when one steals from another or accuses one of stealing from another. I'm suddenly conscious of storytelling—that often the version of events told by students to their parents after they are at home may have little to do with the actual classroom events or my perception of them. All this is stuff they can't teach you in books—such as the "S" factor (surprise), the "H" factor (hormone), and the "R" factor (rebellion). What do I do when a child writes she has a gun in her piano bench? It's all too overwhelming to discuss in one meeting with Sid.

I write my questions down to save them. I dash off a question on my breakfast napkin before work. I scribble them at night to clear my mind for sleep. The writing anchors my thoughts, which otherwise would roam the labyrinth my mind has become, and I can again focus on reading books, planning lessons, and facing the fresh faces again tomorrow. I record my thoughts and vent emotions in words I think but would never say to children or the teachers with whom I work.

Writing in a log heightens my ability to notice things and stretch for the language I need to describe them. I record interesting practices and jot questions I might ask if I had a chance. I observe that some teachers keep a log—but that their journal-keeping takes different forms. Some teachers write copiously about what happened in class, how that specific lesson went, and where they need to explore the next day. Included might be other specifics such as what homework was assigned, the dates of these assignments, and the dates the work is due. Some teachers keep a record in their logs about students who are constantly disruptive. This documentation will become handy if and when intervention is sought.

My log is not yet so concrete. My entries are still full of musings, wonderings, and the big questions that I wrestle with and will help me figure out what my teaching voice is. The practical matters I scribble within the tiny boxes of my plan book alongside the title of the lesson plan and scheduled activities. Even as the first quarter of the year closes and I've got to get report card grades and comments about students together, I find myself short on documentation and must spend time revisiting work folders and student notebooks. I learn quickly that good note-taking of all sorts will make report cards easier. It's also a good idea, I learn, to keep a running tab on all assignments with their dates for the times a parent will ask for a list of all missing homework or the work the child has not accomplished.

Maureen: Seeking Advice from Colleagues

Sometimes it is not enough to record my worries and what I notice other teachers doing. I need to act. So I begin to seek counsel from my colleagues. At first, I ask a "what would you do" question at lunch, rolling the question off as if in easy meandering conversation. But in a moment of urgency I ask another teacher what to do about that child who wrote in an essay she has a gun in her piano bench.

"You must tell the principal," she advises. "Can you imagine the headlines tomorrow if some injury should happen with that gun? The tabloids would scream 'And the teacher knew!'"

Together we amble to the general office. She stands by me as I relate the issue to our principal. She stands over me to make sure that I follow up and phone the parent. She remains by my side to witness the one side of the conversation she can hear—mine. I jot notes in my planner, the date of the conversation and a summary of what is said. I am nervous. The mother tells me not to worry; it's nothing. I hesitate. She says she'll remove it. I don't believe her, but I accept what she says and hang up. I want more reassurance. I want to go to her house with a police officer. But I don't. I create a paper trail. I go home and hug my children and pour myself a drink.

While that colleague offered me solid guidance, support, and solace, asking advice from a fellow teacher can be dubious. I'm not quite sure if the advice provided is trustworthy or, if it is, if it's right for me. Teachers tend to maintain a singular vision. They gravitate to one issue, one classroom, and see through that one lens. But all the staff members in my school have been generous and ready to dole out their best recommendations.

Still, I wonder, whose position do staff members really advocate here at school? For example, one day on leaving the school I see two boys across the street from school punching each other. They are surrounded by a circle of boys urging them on. I recognize the fighters—they're mine. They are an odd match: one white and very tall, and the other black and very short. Both are eighth graders. I cross the street wondering if I should be doing this, thinking about what I'll do when I get there, worried about what will happen. What keeps my legs moving is that they are "my boys" and they look so little to me. A store owner comes out of his store to yell at the boys to stop, and I call them by their first and last names. They look up, and I shout, "Go home!" They focus on my face, and I think they are more afraid of me than each other. They stop fighting, and I keep saying their names in a loud voice, hoping that will bring them back to their sense of themselves, to an understanding that they shouldn't be punching each other. Then I shout the names of all the boys in the ring—seventh graders who, ironically, had just been involved in a workshop sponsored by the district on school violence—to go home. And they do. I'm not sure what I would have done if I had seen the flash of a knife or a metal barrel of a gun.

I walk to my car, my face flushed, burning with anger, with the heat of the words scorching my throat. As soon as I reach home, I phone both boys' mothers. (A teacher had advised me not to call parents from home since so many families have caller identification.) I am able to reach one of them, and she is grateful.

The next morning I ask other teachers if I did the right thing. "Had you gotten hurt, you would have done the wrong thing," is the response from the teacher who is our union leader. Later, a senior teacher and one of the founders of the school comes up to me and whispers, "If I heard you didn't stop the fight, I would have been disappointed." Each reaction reflects a particular position in the school universe. But then, can anyone really provide an answer? What should I have done? I acted without thinking. I was curious at first: I wanted to see what was going on. I saw two boys who were in my homeroom. I did not fear them. The boys looked so young to me at that moment. I reacted like a parent of small children first. It was later, during the car ride home, that I recalled the story of how a teacher I knew got beat bloody stepping between a fight—at an elite high school.

The next morning there was the ritual slamming of the lockers in the hallway but with a wave of whispers: "Mrs. Robins stopped a fight." What were they really saying? I record this incident in my journal and conclude: "There is a lot I have to get used to."

When Sid reads this entry in my log, he writes: "You were being the adult they needed."

I consider this. Later, the senior teacher suggests the idea that I could have lunch with kids in my class. They could bring money so I could take them to a nearby fast-food place, or we could lunch in my classroom. I begin to see her agenda, which initially was expressed to me as advice. As one of the founding members of the school she wants to send a clear message to me about, as Sid comments, being the adult they need.

The next week I pass out a sign-up sheet for "Go to Lunch with Mrs. Robins Fridays." Two or three sign up first. Word gets around. The sign-up sheet grows longer the next week—and I don't care if it's because they prefer fast food to school lunch.

Sid: Encouraging Reflection

Maureen, like all new teachers, craves certainty in an uncertain world. "If a student disrupts the class, what do I do?" "If someone curses, what do I do?" "If I see a pupil cheating, what do I do?" I'm looked to as Solomon— all-knowing, omniscient, the repository of all the right answers. Part of me wishes it were so, but it is not. I know the words I offer cannot be formulaic or automatic.

In every case in which a teacher looks to me for the right answer, I'm tempted to give direct advice, but mostly I don't. It's only when I see someone in total despair pleading for a concrete suggestion that I offer an idea knowing full well that what I say is not a final answer. What the teacher says or does depends on the situation. Key to her response to deviance is her emotional reaction to the event. In the face of aberrant behavior the teacher needs to manage her own feelings. Does the teacher become personally affronted by the use of profanity? Is she angered by the appearance of cheating? Does she feel fear as she approaches two fighting boys?

I point out to Maureen that in her response to the after-school battle she was aware of her lack of fear, and her actions, authoritative and direct, came from a feeling that they were "her boys" and she needed to stop them.

But the issue of fighting is not one restricted to one afternoon's event. In her log Maureen wonders about what she can do to handle the periodic battles that occur. She writes, "As a teacher, I feel overwhelmed by the TV culture of violence. I ask, what is my one little book, one little short story, the one period where we talk about other ways to handle problems going to do. Will they change even one kid when they see on their TV shows that beating up people is the way to success?"

We talk about fights, the reasons they occur, when they're most likely to happen, who gets involved, and what you can do about them. The reasons for fighting are not difficult for us to uncover. When children grow up in neighborhoods and homes where aggressive behavior is the approved way of dealing with difficulty, fighting often is the result. When youngsters see adults using fists to settle problems, they may very likely imitate them. When adolescents have had to use fighting as a means of self-protection, it is not surprising that they use it as a method for dealing with trouble in school. And then when Maureen and I review what she has written in her log, we recognize that we live with movies and television programs that glorify fighting, where peaceful approaches to solving problems are, in the words of the kids, for "wimps and wusses."

We consider when fights are most likely to break out. We agree that it is after gym period of free play or competitive games that the turmoil of activity or bitterness at a lost contest causes pushing and shoving, leading to fights. We also note that dismissals are a time when pent-up emotions and frustration erupt as crowds of youngsters burst forth from the school building.

Together we come up with ideas about what can be done to deal with fighting. Have a few teachers strategically placed outside the building as students leave for the day. Stagger the time for dismissals. Suggest to teachers that they plan a calming activity after students have been in the gymnasium or cafeteria.

I share with Maureen what I've observed other teachers do. One made use of the advisory period to have students talk about the things that bother them. She saw it as a way of releasing anger before it takes the form of fighting. Another indicated that she let students know that she respected their right to be angry when they feel they've been unjustly treated. But she went on to urge the use of words rather than fists to handle the situation. I.S. 250, like other middle schools, has implemented peer mediation and antiviolence programs in the effort to move students from fighting to reasoned discourse. The greatest deterrent to fighting in the classroom is an atmosphere in which youngsters feel a strong identity with the teacher and are involved in satisfying activity.

There are different forms of deviant behavior about which Maureen and other new teachers may need to think: cheating, cursing, stealing, defiance. Finding ways to deal with these problems takes time but they are less likely to occur when students feel the security of clear expectation patterns and have a strong identity with the teacher.

But always my goal is to help Maureen understand the causes of certain kinds of behavior, to develop an awareness of her own personal responses, and to select the action appropriate to the child and the situation. I know that for Maureen to grow as a professional and find her teaching voice, she needs to have someone actively listen.

CHAPTER 3

In the Classroom: Trying Methods from a Book

Maureen: The Anxiety of Observation

After a few meetings with Sid, my rush of questions finally abates. I'm beginning to look closely at my students. I want to plan lessons to meet their particular needs, but I'm not quite sure how. I get to know my students one by one through quiet lunches together or during our school's advisory period, and I get glimpses of the tender personalities behind their public swagger. I worry about a few of them, those that are not loved enough at home, or who are left alone too much of the time by their hard-working parents. I imagine goals for each of them and begin to see them as individuals rather than as members of a group. I tell Sid I'm not used to the emotional demands of being a teacher. In my log I write, "the emotional intensity of my first year...it's as if I'm in my first serious relationship, as if it's the experience of first love." When I discuss this with Sid, he says he knows what I mean.

As I confide this to him, I unknowingly have taken him into my confidence. Trust between us is growing. Sid puts my experience in context and labels it "normal." He confirms my belief that teaching is not mechanical or scripted or predictable. It is not exclusively a brain thing. It's also a heart thing. A psychologist once told me that therapy only works if the client bonds with his therapist. It is similarly true for a teacher and her charges. And it is true for mentor and mentee. That Sid cares about me, about my workload, the way I navigate through my day is evident in tone and conversation, and our relationship has grown to prove it.

Knowing that Sid is behind me, listening to my endless descriptions of classroom situations and lesson planning, enables me to coexist with this

33

feeling of drowning and being pulled in a variety of directions by an imaginary undertow. I feel overwhelmed by all there is to do—the lesson planning, the meetings, student work that needs to be read and assessed, and extracurricular tutoring and activities. Most days I am proud to feel as though I'm treading water, keeping my head above the waterline.

Still, despite the growing confidence I have in Sid as my mentor, our meetings promise work and work demands more time. As the memory of last Wednesday's meeting fades, our next encounter looms large in my consciousness. Not only is there more work, there's also anxiety. I know that Sid will observe me in my classroom. It is an uncomfortable thought.

I've been observed before by a student teacher supervisor and it's no fun. She commented on things like standing with crossed arms and not circulating enough around the room, that I shouldn't repeat what the children said, but interpret and refocus, and I should get the children to respond to each other not just to me. She explored what "teachable moments" are and whether or not we exploited them to our best advantage. During the activity part of the lesson she walked around the room interacting with the students and asking, "What are you doing? Do you understand the directions?" She assessed their work to see how well I'd given instructions. Experienced teachers tell me you never get used to someone observing you—especially if you don't have visitors regularly in the room. There is that anxiety about someone taking notes, looking around, sitting in judgment. You can't help but wonder as you talk to the class what the supervisor in the back of the room is writing, how she is interpreting what you're doing. You feel as though someone is watching your every move—and she is.

There is another level to my concern about being observed by Sid. If he makes suggestions for changes, it's as if I'm doing something wrong. I don't want to be doing anything wrong, though I know I might be. It's something about pride, I guess. Wanting to take that first-year idealism and blow any veteran teacher, and kid, away with my passion for the subject. How naïve!

My struggle to become an effective teacher is mostly internal. It takes the form of self-criticism and rethinking. If things don't go as well as I hope—and often they don't—I try again. I tell myself I'll be better next year, or when I try this unit of study again, or after I consult some books on teaching methods. I try to teach things that I love, and it's painful if they are not received by the kids with welcoming arms. The effort to teach, to impart knowledge, to convey an idea or a concept, to convince an adolescent that learning is important is so very personal and demands incredible interpersonal skills. Knowing this now makes me feel vulnerable, that I don't have the tools I need to do my job adequately. If my students don't seem to be getting it, don't seem to be behaving, I take it very personally.

Often I feel as though I failed.

While all this is going on in my head, my first observation with my principal is scheduled. I ask my colleagues what it will be like, and they tell me not to worry. I prepare my best lesson for the observation. I tell my students the principal is coming to observe *them*, not *me*. On the day of the observation, I dress in my best outfit. It feels to me more like a show, not a means for further professional development.

But I'm lucky. My principal creates a nonthreatening atmosphere and tries to be supportive. Some of my first-year colleagues in other schools worry that their principals will observe them harshly, with a me-versus-them attitude, and the experience of observation will be humiliating and demeaning. Some of my colleagues also worry their mentors will report back to their principals with negative assessments. Another first-year teacher tells me that she has been assigned a mentor who disagrees with the principal's educational philosophy. She must take direction from two divergent sources and this makes for a stressful and uncomfortable situation.

I'm really lucky to have none of that going on. I'm simply worried about Sid witnessing my successes and failures. Actually, I can't imagine my failures or the way in which I might fail. I'm total positivity, full of dreams, full of imagined lesson plans and lesson plans on paper, all geared to the perfectly open student. I want to take all the ideas that I've been thinking about and try them out without someone watching me. I'm fragile at the same time that I am blindly courageous. I think I'll have it exactly right, and I'm just a bit surprised when the kids don't do what I want. At that moment of confusion, crushed pride, and lopsided effort, I don't think I'd appreciate my mentor sitting in back of the room.

Sid: The Ways of Observing

Maureen and I plan for me to sit in on her class the following week, to get a feel for the environment, to see the interaction between Maureen and her students. I make the purpose of my visit clear. I'm bothered by the term *observation*, which is the one used all the time to describe the occasions on which a supervisor comes to a room to evaluate a teacher. It smacks of a scientist looking at a specimen through a microscope. For me a key word is *purpose*. It represents an idea I come back to frequently.

Before I begin sitting in on Maureen's class as observer, I think about what it means for someone to come to a teacher's room to look at what she says and does and how students react. I know in school districts everywhere superintendents mandate that principals observe teachers a set number of times during a semester. In each school the procedure repeats: an administrator armed with a pad and pencil slides to the back of the room to record comments. In my preparation for the New York City principals' examination we were instructed to list as many negatives as we could find to provide grist for postlesson discussion. I spent hours studying mnemonics and memorizing the rights and wrongs of teacher performance. I wondered if this is the mind-set with which supervisors observe teachers.

A vision comes to mind of my first principal opening my classroom door, silently moving into my domain, tight-lipped, grim-faced, pen in hand, poised to assess my worth as a teacher. My students and I had spent days preparing for the visit, decorating the bulletin boards, organizing the bookshelves, and making sure the floors would be free of paper.

I heard myself talking too fast, too loudly, as I strove to will my students into shining brightly and reflecting my skills as teacher before the judging figure in back of the room. Sensing that I was on display, the children rallied to my support, not calling out, participating actively, as they cast secret looks at the stranger in their midst.

After the lesson, my principal moved out of the room as wordlessly as he had entered. As the door closed behind him, I became aware of a dryness in my mouth and of a weight lifting from my shoulders. It's no fun having someone watching your every move and scribbling comments on a yellow pad.

A few days later I received three copies of a report, one for my files, one for the superintendent's records, and one for the principal's office files, indicating areas I had handled well and items in need of improvement. I signed all three and a history of my professional development had begun.

I reflect on my own experience to keep tuned in to how a new teacher feels while being observed and to resist any inclination to follow automatically what coaching courses for principals, district office fiats, and Board of Education memoranda on mentorships have prescribed as the way to improve classroom instruction. I know that formal observations are only a small part of what a supervisor or mentor does to help a teacher to grow. But they are a part of reality, and if they are going to be of use, I want them to help nurture my relationship with Maureen. I don't want to go mechanically through the steps of a preobservation meeting, the classroom observation, a postobservation conference, and a final written summary of the experience to be buried in a supervisor's files. I don't want to be like the principal who distributes a checklist outlining expectations and then in meetings with the teacher discusses how well the teacher did on the listed items. I don't want to be the silent interloper who enters a room to note if the floor is free of waste paper and books on shelves are neatly arranged. I don't want to be part of a performance in which a teacher daily admonishes the class to be on its best behavior when the principal appears, and weeks

before the scheduled event, has students scurrying around preparing bulletin boards. I remember when I was studying to be a supervisor and I'd
express to my colleagues how meaningless the observation process seemed
to me, they'd say, "Wait until you become a supervisor. You'll do exactly as
the rest of them do." I promised myself that would not be the case. I don't
want to see a show put on for my benefit.

Observations will take place when Maureen feels some sense of comfort
about my being in her classroom. In time, as I appear in her room every week,
not only to be the observer but to work with her and to participate with the
children, I hope she'll feel easier about my presence. Each time I visit her
classroom it will be with a focus on questions we've decided on together. I
intend for us to meet after each observation to review what has happened, to
discuss how the problems we've posed have been handled. These will be
meetings of sharing, not telling. I'll reiterate the purposes of the observation,
probe with further questions, offer suggestions, summarize our findings, and,
as I do, affirm my belief in Maureen's ability and intelligence.

Maureen: The Power of Seeing

I agree that Sid can come to observe. I have come to trust him. I know
that whatever transpires between us will remain confidential, that he is my
supporter, not reporter. Still, I want to make sure he sees me at my best. I
can only bear to hear what I might be doing right. I select my best class,
eighth graders. They are a bright, motivated bunch, with many aspiring to
admission to leading New York City high schools like the Bronx High
School of Science, Stuyvesant, or Townsend Harris. The least risk. For one
thing, the kids behave and a small group goes the extra mile inspiring some
positive academic competition. Above all, they are kids who still see that a
good education is the route to a decent life.

My lesson plan does not seem complicated. I'll review the just published—and difficult to decipher—rubrics for the brand new English
Language Arts test administered by New York State. Afterwards, I'll divide
the group into discussion circles of three or four students. I had never really done this with the class before, but I think it will be a good lesson to show
Sid. In planning for my mentor, I am still thinking about the "show" part of
the observation. I want him to see that I'm using varied methods. I want
him to see that I'm up on the latest ideas in education.

The focus of discussion was to be several pages from the challenging-
for-eighth-graders novel, *The House of the Seven Gables* by Nathaniel
Hawthorne. To insure that the discussion groups run smoothly and students
stay on task, I came armed with xeroxed forms from Harvey Daniels's book

Literature Circles: Voice and Choice in the Student-Centered Classroom (1994) outlining specific roles and tasks for students engaging in literary discussion. The roles include "discussion director," "vocabularian," "illustrator," and others. If they assume the roles as prescribed on the sheet, they'll focus on issues in the book and address the general themes along with specific details from the text.

It worked well when my fellow education students tried it for the first time in class at the college. Why shouldn't it work well with a group of intelligent, motivated youngsters?

The eighth graders are eager to participate and showcase their knowledge in front of Sid. They also want to ace the spring test so they listen attentively as I explain the format of the new exam. I stand in front of the room and suddenly, with Sid present, become aware of my stance as the students bullet me with questions. While I respond as best I can, I become increasingly panicked about my stance. I am with the class, talking, responding, but I am also anticipating Sid's comments. I imagine our debriefing: "Why were you standing with your arms crossed?" "Why didn't you circulate as you answered questions?" "Why didn't you write an aim on the board?" I begin to feel my control over the class weaken.

Questions about the test die down, and I am ready to make the transition to group work. But when we move to the unpracticed roles for discussion, there is confusion, an unwillingness to get out of chairs, to shift modes. Sid drags a chair to one group and listens in. I roam around the room observing the conversations. One group scrambles to understand their task, but others are conversing about their favorite rock groups. Soon it becomes apparent that most of the them had not read the assigned section of the novel. I grow nervous.

I pretend to join one of the other groups. I say "pretend" because I'm watching Sid watch me and the students. I simply can't concentrate. So many things are going wrong. If Sid weren't there, I might have asked the class to shut their books and read aloud in round robin fashion—something that I loathe. Later, I gather from other teachers that it takes much practice and training to get kids to work well in small groups, let alone getting them to know specific roles. But now I am a bundle of emotions, angry at the students for not doing their homework, embarrassed at feeling "revealed" as a fake, someone who doesn't know how to teach. I begin muttering to myself a phrase that would become my mantra: "I'll be better next year!"

Sid: The Gentle Intruder

I want to make Maureen feel comfortable with me in her classroom. But I wonder whether ease can ever be achieved when in the past if someone came into your class, it was for the purpose of evaluating, of gauging ability, of judging worth. Prior to my visit I had suggested that Maureen introduce me as someone interested in seeing how the class worked together. I was not hopeful that my words would erase her feelings of discomfort.

I join Maureen's eighth-grade class where they're all reading Nathaniel Hawthorne's *The House of the Seven Gables*. Student heads tilt in my direction. Who is this stranger? They cast secret glances at me. Does my presence change the chemistry of the class? Will what I see represent anything at all like how things usually operate?

I look around to get a sense of the space in which Maureen and her students spend their day. I want to share in her experience so that we have a basis for discussing what goes on. The class is situated in a corner of a large area. Five or six adolescents in wooden chairs around each of four tables. A small blackboard is available for Maureen's use. A large teacher's desk covered with papers and scattered books fronts the room. A bank of computers sits against one wall of the class. I see teenage youngsters needing to expend energy, to explore, and to walk around, crowded in on each other. The reality of the physical space makes for a class that relies on talk for instruction rather than activity. To be in Maureen's classroom is to realize that she works with real handicaps.

During the discussion that follows, all the responses are directed at the teacher as she stands in front of the group asking questions. I see the attention of the class wandering. Some respond with puzzled looks to the information outlined on the forms Maureen has distributed. Others probe their neighbors with the question, "What are we supposed to do?" It's only when talk returns to forthcoming tests that eyes focus on the teacher. In time, after some confusion, the students move into small groups and attempt to deal with the outlined assignments. I go to one of the tables. It becomes apparent that most of them have not read the assigned section of the novel. One who has done the reading takes on the discussion director role while others become the resident artists and begin to sketch out images of the House with its elaborate trees and gables. The period ends without Maureen having an opportunity to review what has been done.

After class, we head to a nearby fast-food place for lunch and talk. What to discuss? I don't want to follow the usual supervisory pattern of enumerating the positive qualities of the lesson and then coming up with a series of suggestions for improvement. I know that teachers have become so inured to this standard approach that they often tune out the beginning of the discussion and wait anxiously for the criticism to come. I need first to deal with Maureen's concerns, which I see mirrored in her furrowed brow, that the class hadn't gone the way she would have liked.

Maureen tells me that the stress on tests is driving the kids crazy. She goes on to say, "The push for standards has put me and my students on a march to read a set number of books without stopping to love them. The things we're doing are more suited to a factory than a school." She wonders whether her students are reading at home, whether they fake responses in class discussions without having read the book. She talks about her attempts to have students analyze stories by querying them about plot development, use of details, introductory sentences. She is doing what teachers all over the city are doing as they join the drive to implement standards.

I'm troubled by the effort to scientize educational approaches. Instead of absorbing the experience of reading a book, the tendency is to become engrossed in the analysis of the experience. Learning is becoming paper driven (list the main ideas; record the number of books you've read; write down all the words that describe a character).

I look back to other times in which slogans rather than thought directed how schools were to work. "New math," "back-to-basics," "outcome-based education," "open classrooms," "standards-based instruction" rule the roost for a while, only in time to retreat into the background. I remember at the college level collecting lists of "competency-based objectives" intended to guide class instruction, which soon became lost in unread files. All of these approaches may have had a sound basis, but all fell victim to the fact that programs established without student and teacher participation lead, at best, to superficial application. I worry about the danger of the current fad becoming the force propelling educational programs.

I go to the Board of Education Bulletin on Performance Standards (1997). In the section on English it states: "Read 25 books of the quality and complexity illustrated in the sample reading list." I would rather put it this way: "Read books that stimulate your curiosity, your interest. Read them with your feelings, your ideas on how they connect to your life. Notice how the writer presents his or her thoughts. Share your reactions with your friends, your classmates, your family" (p. 23).

Maureen has tried to follow the guidelines, and her frustration shows when she says, "Reading for them is just work. They think I'm a crackpot because of the way I push books." She asks, "How can you get children excited about reading? Can you force someone to love something?"

We talk about what can be done to turn adolescents into readers. We discuss our own reading experiences. Maureen tells me about her daughter, whose early years were spent in a hospital. "Jackie was fascinated with *Curious George Goes to the Hospital*. She couldn't get enough of it."

Together we explore ways of connecting books to children's lives. We realize we're competing with television, movies, and a society where students move to an MTV beat. But maybe our excitement, enthusiasm, and love of books can create an oasis of caring about what books can tell us. Maybe if we give students access to lots of different books with different levels of difficulty and allow them to select the ones they want to read, they'll catch the habit of reading. Maybe they'll begin to look at reading more as fun, as an intriguing activity rather than as another instance of mandated schoolwork.

I remember my own teaching days when every second Wednesday I'd pile as many of my pupils as could fit into my old Chevy for our biweekly trip to the Queensborough Public Library where, in the absence of a school library, we'd all take out our full measure of 10 books each to bring back to our classroom to share with others. I realize now how in my eagerness to get books into my classroom I ignored the boundaries of legality. I'm sure I received parental notes of permission to take the children in my car, but I probably left myself open to liability in case of an accident. But we never lost a book, and my students learned to love to read. Forty years later an ex-student wrote reminding me of how our fourth-grade class together built a world of books:

> There we'd be on those Wednesdays extending the school day, enlarging its borders. This "we" I refer to were as many of my class-mates as could safely squeeze into his Chevy. Under our chins arm-loads of books were piled, the books that had been borrowed on the last Wednesday trip. We were thrilled to have library cards so we could have our pick, ten books each. The purpose of these trips was for us to create an ever-changing library in our classroom. Each of us would bring back our book choices for the next two weeks to be bor-rowed and taken home by our classmates. Reading was the order of the day with sheer quantity reveled in, with all the books ours for devouring, with literature holding sway in our class. . . . There were forty students in my fourth-grade class, so I didn't get to go to the library every time. Still, that year I read an awful lot of books.

I tell Maureen I've just finished Philip Roth's *The Human Stain* and ask what she's been reading. We start a practice at each of our sessions of talk-ing about our own reading, and thinking together what made us kids who before sleep put our books under our pillows so that we could return to the imaginative world of literature the first thing in the morning, who relished periods in schools of free reading, who loved the smell of libraries. I see con-tradiction in schools of teachers loaded down with paper work and extra duties who are pressured to improve test scores in reading and never find the time to read themselves.

Maureen: Working One on One

What I'm finding so difficult about working with a mentor is that whatever comfort level I've established in the classroom is constantly being nudged away. Nothing remains unexamined, nothing remains excluded from consideration. There is no buffer between Sid and me, no other student teachers to distract him. I remember thinking when I first started working with Sid, "Great! I have him all to myself without the other interns to dilute our relationship." I've talked and talked and talked. Now it's time to work on my teaching techniques, my classroom demeanor, my management skills, and this work is very difficult.

Sometimes I'm not ready to bare myself to this weekly identification of weaknesses and strengths. Even my journal, which at one point was my lifeline, is becoming difficult for me to maintain. It is no longer a matter of only listing or jotting observations. Now I must slow down and be thoughtful, focused, and specific. Each week I tell myself there are things I have to consider doing differently.

When Sid leaves after our Wednesday meetings, I feel as though I've been through the wringer. He wants to address educational issues and how they affect the classroom. He poses big questions that have no right answer but much to consider: how to assess kids, how to develop independent readers, how to conduct a discussion group, how to create memorable times for the students, how to assess individual learning styles, and on and on. This is exhausting. I feel as though he is a personal trainer of the mind, forcing my brain to perform a higher number of sit-ups and leg lifts than the week before.

This is not the experience of other teachers with their mentors. A colleague told me that discussion with his mentor revolved around practical classroom management techniques, such as asking the child who is talking the most to be a monitor. I wondered if that was all mentoring should offer—a classroom trick that works for 30 seconds?

I remain frustrated, however, by the gap between theory and practicality, between what teachers have in their minds, their wishes and aspirations for their students, and how these notions get—or don't get—translated to the class, how teaching is communicated in concrete ways. I have seen brilliant teachers have their lessons stomped on by kids and end up branded as "ineffective." On the other hand, less intelligent teachers are able to hold a class in the palm of their hands with little apparent effort. It's hard to figure. Teacher lore passes down the image of the little old lady bent over with age who walks into a room and immediately creates silence, whereas down the hall the young hulking man needs to shout down his ill-mannered charges. It almost makes you think that to be a successful teacher something powerful must radiate from you.

Sid and I talk about this. We've both known little old lady teachers who command a lunchroom of children to order. If we knew what ingredients contributed to her success, we'd bottle it. A teacher may use nonverbal communication to indicate that she means business but that she's also loving and kind. I've learned from Sid that a soft but firm approach is best even when dealing with the most contentious of children.

Sid is always asking if I need help with something related to classroom management, and I say no. Not yet. Because in my stubborn heart I'm hoping that content, the stuff we read, the topics we discuss and debate, will galvanize the students in an ideal and optimal way. I guess it will take years for me to understand that being a teacher is as much about being a leader with a way of seeing and reading the various types of learners within the classroom as it is about being a person who delivers content.

Sid: A Look at Listening

After we talk about how to try to make readers out of adolescents, we return to thinking about the lesson I observed the previous week. Maureen says, "Part of the problem I have with the class is that they don't listen to each other. In advisory sessions they interrupt each other, and in class discussions their minds wander. I never get the feeling that all of them are attending to me or their classmates."

I point out to Maureen that often, when teachers talk about language development, they refer to reading, writing, speaking, and rarely give much attention to listening. We agree that we need to encourage better listening. I ask Maureen to consider how the room has an impact. Many of the youngsters sit facing the heads of others, a situation hardly conducive to careful listening. We discuss getting rid of the teacher's desk and excess furniture. Maureen will place the youngsters in a circle and, as much as she can, sit with them.

We come up with other ideas. Maureen will facilitate group responsibility for attending to others by calling on students to react to what other children say and urging youngsters to indicate if they can't hear someone. I remind her to be alert to the common teacher habit of repeating student answers since that serves as a message to others that there's no need to listen the first time. I also caution her to avoid asking questions by starting with the student's name as that gives others permission not to listen because the query is not directed at them. I tell her about the term *arrow of recitation* to suggest that she encourage students to direct their replies to other students rather than always to her as the teacher.

We brainstorm ways to teach listening skills and develop a list of suggestions:

- Ask the class to be silent and to identify as many different sounds as they can.
- For individual or committee presentations, organize the rest of the class into "listening islands" with different groups responsible for finding the answers to different questions.
- Have the students listen to a piece of music and write down how it makes them feel.
- With the class make a chart listing the characteristics of a good listener.
- Have a discussion with the class about the things that interfere with good listening, such as noise, unclear speech, a mind on other matters, and boring content.

We agree that ongoing attention to improving the way students attend to each other is important and we'll consider additional approaches about how to teach listening. Before we leave the subject, I share my view that also needed are a teacher who models good listening and a classroom atmosphere of caring and respect.

Even though we have discussed the area of listening at some length and will continue to do so, I still have an uncomfortable sense that we haven't given enough attention to specific teaching techniques. We've been spending most of our time discussing ideas. When I look at what other mentors have written in their reports, I note items such as "using technology," "finding the main idea," and "correct usage." Maybe I should be focusing on establishing the lesson aim, doing a medial summary, or homework-checking routines. I feel a pressure to be the bureaucracy's good soldier, to do all the things prescribed in the Board of Education's memorandum on mentoring, to arrange each week for a demonstration lesson, a class observation, and an intervisitation.

Just as I urge Maureen to reflect on what she does as a teacher, I also, as her mentor, need periodically to assess whether or not I am effective in my role. I wonder how much I am helping Maureen and whether I am sufficiently connected to the world in which she teaches. I ask myself if I am still able to assist someone to grow as a professional, even though it's been a long time since I've been a public school teacher and principal.

I've been resisting giving demonstration lessons because I question the value of someone strange to a group teaching a lesson out of the flow of regular class activity. I don't believe it helps a teacher to establish her own teaching style by seeing someone else's style. I also don't want to encourage the idea that a "stand-up-in-front of the class" demonstration represents the preferred approach to teaching.

I consider if my hesitancy to put myself in front of a group of adolescents comes from doubts about my ability to do an effective job of teaching. I tell myself that to mentor doesn't mean I have to be the perfect teacher, someone who does everything right and never makes a mistake. Joe Torre can instruct a Yankee on hitting technique without facing a batter. Herman Edwards can show Wayne Chrebet how to run a pass pattern without doing it himself.

Even though we do not begin a regular schedule of demonstration lessons, I do not rule them out entirely since they may help to open discussion about handling routines, ways to ask questions, the use of voice, and other topics. But always the focus is on how Maureen sees herself as a teacher and how she reacts to children.

The next day I receive an e-mail from Maureen. She describes something she never tried before, an approach in which she gave her students a great deal of leeway in choosing books and sharing their reactions. They reacted with enthusiasm to the opportunity to talk about their selections and to exchange ideas. The last sentence of her e-mail reassures me: "You see, even if it seems we only talk about philosophy, we can translate that to practical usage."

Maureen's comment causes me to think about what contributes to professional development. In most schools and for most principals, classroom observations comprise the total job of in-service learning. District superintendents support this view as they insist on a prescribed number of supervisory observations for both new and veteran teachers. I agree with Maureen that these scheduled visits often portray performance rather than the reality of the classroom. Classroom observation with cooperatively identified purposes and collaborative follow-up discussion can be helpful. However, it is not the isolated event that makes for teacher growth, but rather the development of a community of stimulating and enthusiastic learners. Teacher growth is nurtured by a learning environment in which there is an ongoing exchange of ideas, books, and articles. As Maureen's mentor, I want to be part of that environment.

Maureen: From Theory into Practice

My entire first year is developing into a series of experiments that are sometimes not conceptualized fully before I perform them. Because Sid and

I have been working out an idea—what makes a good discussion group—I rushed home to unearth some xeroxed forms, which I was given in a graduate course, for "literature circles," a concept I loved. If I tried this for the lesson Sid came to observe, he'd think I was making progress, growing as a teacher, maturing in my instructional thinking.

At this point, I am not really thinking about my students; I am thinking of how Sid will view me. I intend to take the ideas presented in the graduate course, specifically those from Harvey Daniels's book *Literature Circles* (1994), and try to put them into practice. I have not looked at his work with the eyes of an experienced instructor who can break these parts down into kid-friendly steps so that they would be prepared for vigorous discussions about books. A novice cook reads a cookbook differently from someone who knows his way around a recipe. It becomes clear to me that before I attempt something I must look into the nuts and bolts of how to launch it, consider how to have the kids buy in, and, if the new method doesn't go over well, stay with it and give it a chance before giving up. I continue to survey all the methods teachers use and write about.

My first year's path to professional growth is paved with the patchwork of advice about different possible approaches. It is a bumpy road.

Sid: Theory Versus Practice

I witness Maureen's struggle to bridge the chasm that often appears between the good idea and its implementation. I sometimes see her classroom become a scene of combat between the theoretical concepts she has learned in a college classroom or gleaned from a professional book and the reality of her students' reaction to what she proposes. An example of this gap is the lesson in which she tried to get students to work together in small groups to discuss *The House of the Seven Gables*, an idea she had picked up from reading Harvey Daniels's book *Literature Circles* (1994). During the week, I read this book that Maureen has used to help her go about setting up literature circles, and I find it's full of excellent ideas thoughtfully presented. When I next meet with her, we review what happened during my last visit with her class.

Maureen wonders why an approach that worked so well with her fellow education students at the college didn't work as well with a group of intelligent, motivated youngsters. She puzzles over the fact that, even though she had prepared xeroxed forms taken from the book outlining roles and tasks, when students moved into groups, the discussion wandered. While some grappled with the assignment, others were conversing about their favorite rock groups. It soon became clear that most of the class had not read the novel.

As we deal with the lesson itself, we also think about the problems involved in incorporating what seem like worthwhile approaches into the flow of classroom learning. One obstacle to the implementation of a good idea is the tendency of new teachers to "fall in love" with an attractive method and rush to try it out in their classrooms. Maureen recognizes that she has moved too quickly and that her students were unprepared to take on the different roles identified for carrying on a book discussion.

We talk about items meriting consideration before thrusting her students into book discussion clusters. For example, the purpose of the sheets describing the roles of discussion director, vocabularian, illustrator, and others ought to be established beforehand. The class needs to understand that the xeroxed forms exist to spark conversation and not provide the bulk of talk. Time should be provided for an exchange of views about the kinds of questions a discussion director might ask and to explore the way people in other roles might best function. The teacher needs to think about how best to assign students to groups so that varied ability levels are represented.

Maureen and I agree that the idea of literature circles is interesting and Daniels's book provides useful suggestions on how to implement them. But even with careful, thoughtful application of the ideas presented in the book there is no guarantee that the approach will work out successfully in the classroom. To believe that you can take recommendations offered in a book, at a workshop, or in a college course and have them unfailingly work in a public school classroom is to fail to recognize the complexity of the teaching act. It is to look at theory as absolute truth and not see that no theory is able to cast a wide enough net to encompass all the factors influencing the teaching/learning process. It is for us, the teacher and her mentor, to examine the theoretical concept and to adapt it so that it applies to the situation in which we are working. But even the way it is modified is affected by the students' prior attitudes toward books, the teacher's enthusiasm, the materials available, the physical setup of the room, the classroom atmosphere, the time of the day the idea is introduced, the quality of student-teacher relationships, the pupil's role in selecting the literature, and other elements about which we may not even be aware.

This is not to suggest that teachers should not avail themselves of ideas coming from books, courses, and seminars, but teachers should realize that when it comes to different classrooms in different schools, the same strategy or the one way of doing things will not work every time with every student. To believe you can take an idea and implement it in a mechanical fashion is to denude the teaching act of its artistry.

I share with Maureen my view that successful teaching takes more than intellectual excellence or technical prowess. There are internal qualities needed such as optimism, resilience, initiative, adaptability, and abilities belonging to the creative artist that are hard to define. I think to myself that as Maureen's mentor, as her supporter and encourager, I want to help her uncover and strengthen those characteristics.

CHAPTER 4

The Lesson That Fails

Maureen: My Most Difficult Class

I complained to Sid over and over how sometimes I feel artificial, a representation of some one I am not, and he has inspired me to try to be more like the real me in the classroom. I love talking about books, and he has encouraged me to discuss books with kids. As we confer about how to get kids to talk about books, we are also addressing my need to find my teaching voice. Sid reminds me to consider what I enjoy doing at home with my own children that I could transfer to my classroom.

I often chat about books at home with my daughters. They enjoy their book talks with me because they know I'm extremely interested in hearing what they have to say. I lean forward to make sure I hear them. I concentrate on their words. I respond to one of their comments while the other listens and jumps in when she connects to what is being said. Even though they are different ages, Elizabeth, my older daughter, will often read to her younger sibling so that they can both talk about the book together. There is love underlying our conversation. I want to bring them along in their thinking, to look at books closely. At home, not only do I model conversation about books, but I model my life as a reader. My daughters constantly see me with my nose in a book—so much so that they have learned to snap it shut when they need attention.

I have also learned from my daughters that they are different types of readers and they read for different purposes. Elizabeth loves to lose herself in faraway places. Jackie, my younger child, likes to read for information, about major surgery she had as a baby. Through *Curious George Goes to the Hospital* by H.A. Rey, she could put a name to the place in which she had spent so much time, which until then was an experience that floated around in her mind without the names or words to describe it. During our first reading Jackie blurted, "I know this place! I've had x-rays too!" We read that book many times, and she would wait for me to collect myself at the moment when the Man with the Yellow Hat has to leave George by himself in the hospital. Not long afterwards, Jackie found another soulmate in *Madeline* (1939). After an operation, she had a scar on her belly too.

I think and reflect in my log about what I do at home with my daughters and how I can bring what I do at home into my classroom.

"We have to model how to talk about books with kids," Sid says. "How do you find out about books you might want to read? You talk to friends who tell you what they've been reading. You share your excitement about the story, the ideas, or the writer's style." He's right. I often hear about books that might interest me from friends.

After our last meeting I selected 10 of my favorite books from my classroom shelves and lined them up on the ledge of the chalkboard before my students came in. When they entered the room they began buzzing to each other asking, "Why does she have those books lined up?" Anything that's a departure from routine in the room is cause for conversation and curiosity. After they were all seated, I began to tell them why there were books lined up that way and what each book was about. I offered to pass them around and to loan them out. Many wanted to borrow, but since I had only selected 10 not everyone could; the others, I hoped, would browse the shelves and make a selection. The energy of the room was high, and I knew that the work for me would to follow up and sustain the energy.

That group of students supported me in my attempt to speak effectively to them in a voice that was natural to me. When I picture doing a book talk with my most challenging class, I feel intimidated and my courage retreats. I don't want to present my real self. For this class, I display a different persona, a teacher who has a hard shell. I wonder if I had videotaped myself in both classes if I would see myself posed with two completely different body langauges. I'm sure my most challenging class was familiar with my scowl.

Adolescent students can be blunt and talk out loud among themselves about how "poor" the teacher is. Surely, many teenagers have more disposable income than I do, particularly now that I am starting over. If I have to admit it, some of these rude students remind me of those who bullied me when I was in the seventh grade. I want to talk to Sid about finding a different way of connecting with the adolescents—if I can—because right now I've exhausted all I know.

I ask Sid to schedule his observation period when I have my difficult class. If he has to witness me fail and fail miserably as a teacher, so be it.

I meet this class during the last period of the day. It is comprised of students of varying ability. Most of them are troubled readers with short attention spans. There are more boys in the class than girls; often the girls sit frustrated at the misbehavior of their classmates of the opposite sex. Except J. She is trying out her feminine wiles on these almost-men, and they are loving the distraction. When the subject matter requires abstract thinking, they can't remain focused. I have asked around school for advice on what to do with them. The assistant principal suggests that I build a series of lessons with hands-on activities or make use of videos.

Other teachers cope with this group with a variety of strategies that don't always work. The mathematics instructor had the best plan: short periods of instruction, practice problems from the textbook, and review. Predictable classroom structures helped them to stay organized. In Spanish, however, where the teacher is soft-spoken and maintained few rituals, they were always troublesome and acting out. I continue to puzzle about what would be the best way to approach this class.

I know other teachers and writers, such as Nancie Atwell and Lucy Calkins, suggest that reading and writing sessions offer students lots of choice—what to read, where to read, whether by themselves or in pairs. With no place to move and little faith in my troublesome students, that doesn't seem to be a realistic option. I am too quick to dismiss a teaching philosophy that might help me fully articulate my teaching voice. A Reading and Writing Workshop is structured around a minilesson, 8–10 minutes of direct teaching, and time to read or write (depending on the workshop) independently. A time for the full class to share wraps up the session. Workshop teaching is student-centered in that kids work on their own or with a partner at their own level. I search for an answer, but because I don't have the time now, it won't come from Atwell's *In the Middle* (1997), but rather, I hope, from a 3-hour United Federation of Teachers seminar on how to help kids write better. A quick fix—or so I think.

The following Monday I tell this class that we are going to do something new. I ask them to number five lines on their notebook sheets. I write a prompt—a topic that they could respond to—on the board, and they are to write quickly to fill in all five lines. They are agreeable to the challenge of the day. It's almost a game.

Because of this small success I am inflated with optimism and possibility—even if my instinct tells me otherwise. So on Wednesday, the last period of the day, I plan to begin with Part 2 of this writing strategy, which involves asking them to write several lines more for Sid's observation. The class bursts through the door straight from a period of gym. Some are flushed or angry. They are still carrying on a debate over who did what, and if they had done it differently, their team would have won the game. All are thirsty and eager to visit the water fountain. They've got just under an hour before they can go home—and they have to spend 50 minutes with me.

Our open classroom is packed, fully operational that day with four classes going on simultaneously. There is a lot of noise in the room. The troublemakers see Sid and decide that he is there not to observe them, but to observe me. An exercise that yesterday and the day before seemed to grab their goodwill now becomes an opportunity to get under my skin. In addition to the "I don't get it" pronouncements and stalling questions, they begin to chat amongst themselves at their tables. Things are deteriorating by the second. I ask them to read aloud from the novel we are studying. They usually enjoy reading together, but this focuses them only for a minute. I again feel the anxiety of being observed, and my class and lesson plan come grindingly to a halt. In desperation, I do something I might not have done—bring up the topic of yesterday's bomb scare.

On Tuesday, a school secretary received a phone call informing her there was a bomb in the school. She approached each one of us with a brief typewritten note alerting us to the threat and saying that we should calmly and quietly escort our students to another schoolyard two blocks to the northeast. Teachers and students sat on the playground's macadam at the farthest corner of the yard while our principal ran back and forth between this school and our own school transmitting what little information he had. At first we were told we would have to remain outside there for 2 hours. Thankfully, the police came swiftly, searched our building, and gave us the okay to return.

As we returned to the building, one boy asked, partly in concern and partly in an effort to stall getting back to work, "How do they know there isn't a bomb in the lockers?"

"We didn't see any dogs," said another. "How can they be sure?"

Our school lives have become less real and more of the stuff of television. We are rattled and the lingering effect of this threat to our security remains with us. Those skittish about books have their minds on weapons and aggressive behavior. I light upon the bomb experience as a way to grab their attention in front of Sid. I ask them to write about it, offering a nearly inscrutable version of a writing prompt.

F., a smart boy who can carry on an entire conversation with his neighbor while listening to every word I say, instructs me that yesterday's event was a "threat" and not a "scare." I am annoyed that he challenges me on semantics, especially in front of Sid. I begin to plot my revenge but relinquish such ideas as a wave of impotence washes over me.

Others complain that they don't want to write about it or even think about what happened. Actually, neither do I. What I want at that moment is to dismiss them to the gym or detention or phone their parents to come and sit beside them in class. What I want is to set the clocks to whir the seconds away at a faster pace. If Sid had not been there, I would have given them an intricate coloring or writing exercise. Or I would have just let them talk.

Instead, I plod on, experiencing feelings of humiliation and failure. I hear again in my head, "I'll be better next year." I am also angry and I find myself secretly plotting ways to get back at my troublemakers with a tough load of work or some equivalent. But there was still Sid to face. Luckily, we don't have time today to debrief.

Sid: The Lesson That Fails

Another of my tasks is to help Maureen distinguish between a class that goes poorly and her sense of failure as a teacher. The class Maureen invites me to sit in on is a difficult one for her, one she meets the last period of the day, and throughout I could sense her frustration.

Maureen asks the students to write 10 lines on a character in a chapter they were supposed to have read for homework. They begin to write, but concentration soon lapses. A group at one table begins to whisper to each other. Questions seeking clarity come. "What am I supposed to write about them?" "Is it okay to have more than 10 lines?" The noise of voices from the other groups with whom Maureen's students share the large room area becomes more of a distraction. In an effort to refocus the group, she calls upon youngsters to read aloud from the chapter. The students continue their private conversations. She reprimands a few in a vain attempt to bring them together. In desperation she switches assignments and asks the class to write about the bomb scare in the school the previous day. Again she meets resistance. One boy said, "I don't want to think about it." Another asked the inevitable question, "How long does it have to be?"

As I watch, I feel her discomfort. Part of me wishes I weren't there so that Maureen could avoid the embarrassment of things going wrong in front of her mentor. I have the urge to walk to the front of the room, to touch her shoulder, to say, "It's all right. There are days when nothing seems to work."

The hour thankfully comes to an end and I'm sorry we don't have a chance to talk because Maureen has a homeroom group and then must pick up her children.

Later, I read her log. "I can't describe how impotent and ineffective I felt with that class. Part of me was embarrassed that you were there to see how awful everything was and, at the same time, I felt how lucky I am to have you come around, to feel good at all your energy to teach me stuff."

At this point I know what Maureen needs most is for me to shore up her confidence, to reassure. I e-mail her.

I know you left the class yesterday feeling that it was a disaster. I remind you that when students misbehave, it's not always because of something you did or did not do. Sometimes other factors come into play—a fight at home, a reprimand in a previous class, or any number of other reasons.

Days of this sort will never disappear from our experience. The fact is that you have the ability, the intelligence, and the attitude that makes you a rare addition to the school.

I recognize again how different are our roles. I respond from the vantage point of the onlooker, the one who records observations, makes comments on behavior. I remember times when my teaching was on display, someone watching, studying my every move, assessing my worth. How uncomfortable an experience it was.

But I cannot match the intensity of her feeling. I do not go to sleep with the faces of children in my head, with concerns about how they will do on tests, with frustration about not reaching certain kids, with anxiety about whether I will keep my job. I have the luxury of being removed and yet I am not, for I want to feel that I have an impact on Maureen's development as a teacher.

As I watch Maureen struggle with discouragement, I am reminded that the road to professional growth has its rough spots. I recall instances of my own lapses in judgment and displays of inadequate knowledge. As a 24-year-old white teacher, I presumed to lead a class of minority-group youngsters in a discussion of racial prejudice. They stared at me blankly. In my fifth grade I called upon an Israeli boy, new to our country, to read aloud. I still see the embarrassment I caused him. My ignorance of classroom management was apparent when I would focus on one child, instructing him in a mathematical concept while leaving the rest of the class to its own devices. The errors I made, as is the case with most newcomers, would comprise a long list.

I share these tales of my own moments of ineptitude with Maureen. I want her to understand that making mistakes is part of learning how to teach and that feeling discouraged at times is not unusual.

As I look to our next meeting, I think of so many things I want to discuss with Maureen. There is the frustration that arises as she faces the futility of seeking energy for traditional activity from a group of adolescents at the end of a day. We could come back to the idea of purpose and consider why the class was asked to write 10 lines about a character in the book or to read aloud. We could deal with the class's unwillingness to write about the bomb scare.

But when we meet, Maureen is eager to talk about how difficult the last minutes of the day can be with a group of energetic teenagers. "What makes it harder is that I get them right after they've had gym. They come to my class all charged up. The other day I lost my temper and yelled at them. I felt very bad about it."

I remind her of what a colleague had told her. He said, "You don't have to operate like a machine. You're allowed to get angry. You get angry at your children at home, don't you? Same here. You're the same person and what gets you fired up at home gets you fired up at school."

Maureen expresses her puzzlement about how to deal with this group. She has seen what other teachers do, has received advice from the assistant principal, and now has picked up an idea at the professional development course. Nothing seemed right for her.

Together we think about times when the class connected to what was happening. Maureen remembers when she broke the class into groups to discuss different parts of *The New York Times*. The students enjoyed the chance to talk with each other. It was a different kind of class—less teacher talking and more student talking.

She goes on to say, "I've seen that there are fewer classroom management problems when the kids are involved in 'doing'—working on the computer keyboard, playing with the art possibilities of a computer program, learning how to type."

We identify other ways for providing students with active learning opportunities: draw a comic strip depicting major events from the story; make up a list of clues for guessing the name of a book character; prepare to dramatize an incident from the book; role-play an interview with the author of the book.

I stress the importance of preceding writing assignments with much prior discussion. Her attempt to get the class to write about the bomb scare found the students unprepared to deal with the issue. One boy might well have been expressing the attitude of others when he said he didn't want to think about what happened. For writing, particularly for writing of this sort, talk is needed to stimulate thinking, to ignite interest, and to open the way to feelings about what may have been a frightening event.

We agree that different groups call for different approaches, that for students who are unable to organize themselves there may be a need for tight structure. For example, in her attempt to involve the class in the writing exercise she had planned, Maureen would have been well advised to review how the exercise had been done the previous day and to outline again procedures to be followed.

I point out to Maureen that a major theme we've been discussing all year is the disconnect between what we ask youngsters to do and what they want to do. I share with her something Frank McCourt (2002) wrote recalling his experience as a teacher at Peter Stuyvesant High School in New

York City. "There are three main avenues to a teenager's heart: sex, food, and music" (p. 23). He had his students read restaurant reviews and then write their own reactions to lunch in the school cafeteria or dinner at home.

I remind Maureen of a class discussion of *The Giver* (Lowry, 1998) and how animated the youngsters became when they were asked to contrast the parent-child relationship in the book to their own experience with parents. Then there was their involvement in the lesson in which they compared the words in poetry they'd been reading with the lyrics of popular songs. We conclude with the thought that an ongoing task is to search out ideas and materials that connect to children's lives.

Maureen: My Mentor Offers Consolation

I think it was the way Sid nodded his head or the look in his eyes that gave me reassurance that he understood. That I hadn't let him down. That he had seen it before. That he perhaps had done it himself. When I got home I e-mailed him and predicted, correctly this time, that he wanted to tell me that sometimes lessons don't go as planned but that doesn't reflect on my overall abilities as a teacher. Later, when we see each other, we summarize what was observed: that kids at the end of the day need to be active, to do something with their hands. Sid suggests debate, an art project in the service of expanding their understandings of the literature they are engaging. In short, I need to find a way to engage them through active learning.

Sometimes it's a matter of not letting the kids press my buttons. One boy loves to entangle me in verbal combat—because he knows he can. I have come to believe he does this to reenact a relationship with someone he knows outside of school. Sometimes the chemistry is just not there and a teacher doesn't mix well with a particular group. And sometimes it just takes the one or two kids who confound you to disrupt the class, adolescents who need to be on the wrong side of authority. I had to learn how to cope with that. This was the beginning of understanding myself. For one thing, I learned how hot-tempered I can be. Another teacher at school counseled me about this: "You lose your temper at home with your kids right? How else do they get the message of what they can and cannot do?" In the classroom, however, to be effective, to help my students control their own volatility, I need to maintain a more even keel. I also learn the value of rituals, how they can be comforting and make a group feel more safe because they can predict what is going to happen next.

CHAPTER 5

Integrating the Academic with the Personal

Maureen: How Do I Conduct a Discussion Group?

I ask Sid to help me become more adept at conducting a full-class discussion group. It's one thing to moderate a conversation with a group of 4—but 34? What skills do I need for large-group discussion? Because Sid and I have been discussing the value of accountable talk and talk as rehearsal for writing, I want to do more of it more meaningfully in my classroom.

The eighth graders are going to talk about the television shows they watch and develop some critical sensibility about what they view. My students spend a lot of time in front of the TV screen. They have few critical thoughts, no skepticism, no questions about what they see. This passivity spills into my classroom, into their lives, into their judgments, into a depressed spirit and dampened motivation. They don't care to judge if something is well made or poorly made. They don't care if a show is accurate or full of inaccuracy.

My students are assigned to watch a TV show that they normally would never look at and comment on it. They could choose any show from the Food Channel, Discovery Channel, PBS, or a cable news channel. My aim here was to have them get the idea that there are other channels on the dial besides MTV, WB11, or the shows put on by the World Wrestling Federation.

My technique for a full-class discussion is limited to altering the classroom's physical arrangement: I would seat the students in a circle. Luckily, I am cycled out of the big room this day and into a real classroom with movable desks and chairs. Students seated in a circle are more willing to converse and engage each other. In a circle they sit face to face. There are no backs of the head to muffle ideas or their tender expression. I was not think-ing of Sid's idea about pupil-to-pupil discourse or the arrow of recitation; rather I concentrated on the assignment, the provocative questions I might pose, and the anxiety of what they will say with Sid present.

N., the boy I separated from fighting with his classmate earlier in the year, launches the conversation. He says that he watched an interior design show on the Discovery Channel but wouldn't watch it again because he thought the commentator was gay.

Uproar—I expected some surprise but not to this degree. This obser-vation starts out with a bang!

The students, who know each other better than I know them, jump at the opportunity to delve into topics that I rarely hear discussed in an aca-demic environment. They talk about victims and bullies, why certain kids are mean to others, and why students mistreat others. I am shocked, over-whelmed. I try to bring the conversation back to our topic: What did they see in a show they've never watched before? But they persist. I grow increas-ingly uncomfortable with the lack of control I seem to be exhibiting. But I see how much the students want to run with the conversation, all politely taking turns speaking, no one shouting another down, each listening atten-tively to the others. I look over and see Sid, seated in the circle, listening intently, watching the kids, observing how I conduct myself. At first, I am seated within the circle. To assert myself, I stand up to redirect conversa-tion. My arms cross before me—my defensive pose—and I feel the energy now that ebbs and flows through the room like an ocean at high tide.

Sid pointed out in a previous observation that I should avoid repeat-ing what the kids say but rephrase it or redirect it. I become self-conscious with Sid watching that I am not doing that well and that the conversation is getting achingly personal. Should I bring the discussion back to academ-ics? Should I let the kids go where they want? Will Sid think that I am not in control?

As these thoughts pass through my head, I can feel that I have the con-fidence in myself to let things go where they might. This is a good time for risk taking. Sid is here. How could anything go wrong? At this point I am glad he is here, while this class releases much of its stored-up energy.

As I consider how I to wrap up this discussion—in which kids had con-fessed their parents' drug abuse, their sense of being outsiders, their identi-fication with the two boys who killed their Columbine High School class-mates so violently and needlessly in Littleton, Colorado—Sid motions to me with his eyes.

"May I?"

I nod, "Of course." I take an internal deep breath and feel great relief. Sid praises the students for their courage, their honesty. He asks them to reconsider their relationships in light of the ideas they expressed today. He acknowledges their feelings and their efforts. He supports the kids who took chances revealing much more of their inner selves, bringing it into the classroom. Today we send the kids off with something that I alone never could have given them.

For days and weeks later, my eighth graders will talk about this lesson, remind me about what they talked about, and remark, "It was the best day in school we've ever had."

Sid: A Circle of Students

At our last meeting we agreed it might be helpful for me to see how Maureen works as a facilitator of class discussion. I suggested an experiment: "Why not have them sit in a circle and let them participate without raising their hands? Let's see if they can learn to chime in appropriately?" Learning how to have civil discourse, to converse in respectful ways, and to listen to different points of view are real needs for students of this age. All too often their models have been television personalities trading insults, family members arguing rather than sharing, and peers for whom "trash talking" is the norm. We've decided it would be useful to assess with students the quality of their discussions and to have them create a checklist of reminders assessing how well they listen, whether they interrupt, and how they respond to someone with whom they disagree.

I enter the classroom and join a circle of students. The class assignment was to report on a television program they ordinarily wouldn't watch. The ensuing discussion is lively and intense, with interruptions occurring but not so frequently as to disrupt the class.

Issues emerge quickly. N., a small, bespectacled boy, initiates the discussion. "I don't like that home remodeling program because the host looks gay." Almost immediately others pounce on him. "You're talking like a gay basher." "Homosexuals have a right to live." "You don't put them down just because they're gay." N. withdraws into silence unable to counter the onslaught. As I watch him cower before the attacks of his classmates, I have the feeling I want to protect him. At the same time I wonder how to help him look at homosexuals with less hatred, less disdain. A 13-year-old girl, K., suggests, "N. feels uncomfortable around homosexuals. That's why he dislikes them." K. has shown us the way. N. is not going to modify his ideas by being told they're wrong; he is more likely to change if he understands the basis for thinking the way he does.

The students, freed from the strictures of textbooks or formal curriculum, jump into other topics. They begin talking about how people sometimes treat each other badly. The conversation becomes directed at P., a short, frail boy, younger-looking than the others, who is often the butt of his classmates' ridicule. "P. gets picked on because he does silly things." "I get annoyed when he teases." P. squirms but sits silently listening to what is said.

A discussion of the Columbine High School incident ensues. Two girls clad in black with black nail polish and black eye shadow volunteer a thought that startles me. They say they understand the Columbine killers for they know what it is to feel like outsiders. Maureen then asks if others in the class feel like outsiders. Hands come up from three-quarters of the class. I learn later that one of the two girls has an unmarried pregnant sister and the other a father in prison. I am reminded that youngsters bring different agendas with them, that they are the product of different life experiences. It's an idea that I, as mentor, and Maureen, as teacher, recognize we need to keep in mind, not to excuse behavior but to understand it better.

The class was winding up without resolution, but the air had been filled with meaning and excitement. Just as the students are to leave, I ask Maureen for permission to say something. I tell them how much I admire their open expression of feeling and their comments that didn't criticize but helped others to understand.

All week long I can't get the picture of those two girls out of my head, girls who feel so isolated, so much not part of school, so lost that they identify with violence directed at classmates. This session gnaws at me, and later I discuss with Maureen such issues as the problem of developing a sense of community, ways of establishing caring and compassion, and the importance of recognizing the uniqueness of each child.

As we consider ways of creating schools and classrooms that meet the needs of young adolescents, we talk about what makes them tick, what of how they think and feel affects the way they behave. One of the ways we attempt to get inside their heads is to recall our own school experiences when we were teenagers. Maureen remembers entering seventh grade fresh with the injury of her parents' divorce and relocation. I share with Maureen my recollection of my own junior high school days when I felt anonymous, a name in a roll book. Teachers knew little about me except that I did well on tests. They had no idea how ungainly I felt and how, as the child of immigrant parents who spoke with accents, I struggled to feel at ease in an unfamiliar world. Maureen reminds me that many of her students are immigrants and share the same sensibility: shy about speaking for fear of revealing an accent or custom.

When I look back to that time, I think I would have valued having a teacher who talked to me about my interests, my ambitions, and my concerns. I point out to Maureen how her Friday practice of taking a few students to lunch with her provides an opportunity for them to have positive interaction with an adult. I tell her the story of a new teacher in the Harlem school where I had been the principal whose classroom situation improved when the students got to know him as a person, after he played ball with them and chatted with them in the schoolyard during lunchtime. I support what she does to have children explore and express what they are feeling by having them write on such topics as "I feel powerless when...." The practice of keeping diaries or journals also helps in the task of finding a firm identity. The weekly advisory sessions provide another chance for her adolescent youngsters to deal with issues of concern.

As I observed the class discussion, I sensed Maureen's uncertainty about allowing the students to move off into areas that seem nonacademic. She has told me what other teachers have remarked about the concept of advisories: "I've got a curriculum to cover" or "I'm not a psychologist or guidance counselor—what am I supposed to do with what the students say?" I indicate to her how I value her willingness to go beyond traditional approaches to teaching, to be sensitive to her reactions as she did so, and her ability to stay with discomfort. The result was a class in which students explored issues of crucial importance to how they live.

When, a few days later, I read Maureen's comments in her log about admiring the way I summarized the class session, I think about what happened. I reacted spontaneously and sincerely with appreciation for the students' openness and honesty of expression. When we reviewed the lesson further, we agreed that I had given their thoughts and feelings validation, and they left the room having taken part in a discussion they controlled and whose subject matter was meaningful to them.

Maureen and I talk about what to do so that all the youngsters feel a connection to school activity, so that their role as students goes beyond being the passive recipients of a curriculum imposed by others. The opportunity to become involved in such service projects as tutoring younger children and assisting in a nursing home can contribute to a sense of meaningful participation. Maureen reminds me that service learning is a centerpiece of I.S. 250's curriculum and these projects are always close at hand. We can give students a chance to attain a clearer perspective on their own development by studying such topics as adolescence in other countries and eras or adolescence as portrayed on television programs. We agree that we can continue the search for books about those who feel different and unaccepted to aid in creating a more empathic classroom atmosphere.

CHAPTER 6

Other Teachers, Administrators, and the School's Social System

Maureen: The "Outsiders" and School Rules

I think and rethink that class discussion for days. I am profoundly affected by what I learn about my students—and how little I know about the materials I need to bring to their attention. O. Henry short stories exemplifying surprise endings are nice to teach them, but kids need to participate in an ongoing discussion through literature about the issues they face daily. I reflect on my conversation with Sid—how books can help kids expand their capacity to understand themselves and others. What books can I use?

I start with S.E. Hinton's classic teen novel, *The Outsiders*. In that book an adolescent tries to find his way after the loss of his parents. He falls in with a gang, gets involved with murder, runs away, and through a series of losses learns about his place in the world. I read my way through other Young Adult novels by popular writers such as Chris Crutcher and Walter Dean Myers, and I keep in mind what boys would like to read and what girls would like to read. I realize boys tend to like realistic fiction with a touch of fantasy or science fiction; girls tend to love books centered on relationships. I fall in love with Mel Glenn's verse novels, whose stories are articulated by a roster of different characters who rotate throughout—particularly *Who Killed Mr. Chippendale?* (1996) and Laurie Halse Anderson's novel *Speak* (1999). I explore using nonfiction, particularly biography, in the adolescent classroom. I decide Russell Freedman's *Eleanor Roosevelt: A Life of Discovery* (1993) or Jim Murphy's biography of Robert Louis Stevenson, *Across America on an Emigrant Train* (1993) are must-reads for my students—and I'm fortunate to have class sets of each of these great books.

I want my eighth graders to read books that will allow them to feel less alone. Adolescence is such an amalgam of emotions, of being sensitive, of wanting to belong to a group, and of questioning who you are as an individual. I agree with Sid that stories of others in similar situations can be reassuring, and I continue to search for materials to help my students ease their feelings of alienation.

As a first-year teacher, I feel like an outsider too. I empathize with my students, with their concerns about fitting in. I identify with their gawky ways of expressing themselves, their tremendous self-consciousness at trying new things. We are both looking for ways to connect, to be individuals yet linked to a clan.

I'm not yet sure where I belong in the school community. I know the staff saw qualities in me that made them think I would fit in—after all, a committee of parents, teachers, and administrators chose me. I was not someone who transferred in.

The school culture can be described as semi-alternative with traditional hallmarks. There is a different sense of time here at my school. There are no bells. If a class needs more time, all of us are flexible enough to hold on to our classes for extra minutes. It is a far cry from the 42-minute clock of the traditional junior high. Teachers meet with each other regularly, on scheduled common prep time, to plan together when possible and share information about students. I get much more time in the company of my senior colleagues than most first-year teachers. And I benefit from it. Collaboration among colleagues, though, takes a while to develop, and everyone, including myself, remains guarded.

On a personal level, even though I am a teacher, I don't always feel like one. I'm still more student than teacher and often don't recognize myself as the unsmiling, tense adult who stands with arms crossed in front of the classroom. In struggling to define myself as a teacher I have found new patience. But I've also found anger and it expresses itself despite every effort I make to repress it. I shocked myself recently when I hollered, "Are you deaf?" at a troublesome student.

I am trying to become conversant in the language of I.S. 250, its spoken and unspoken rules, its culture. Grasping school rules is a priority. Perhaps it's been so long since they've had a first-year teacher in their midst, none of the staff members reviews school rules, and I rely on common sense to guide me, or I observe what my neighboring teachers do. Like my adolescent charges, I question everything. Why are certain rules in place and who made them? Why can't students wear hats in school? What is the dress code? Who is supposed to enforce it? Are kids allowed to listen to Walkmans? What's wrong with the teenagers having a bottle of water at their desks? Are they permitted to go to the soda machine during the day? Do you limit bathroom passes to one at a time or send them out in pairs?

Often, when a student asks to leave the room, I answer by deferring to another teacher, "Whatever Mr.—— or Mrs. —— thinks." Sometimes I give permission because it makes sense and I have no idea I might be breaking a rule. Some teachers allow only one student out of the room at a time. Others are freer with the pass. I find no schoolwide consistency. I don't know how far some students will go to bend the rules until two boys ask me to go to the bathroom but head for the soda machines instead. They are spotted by the principal. The boys tell him I gave them permission to get a soda to drink in class. The three then amble to my area where I am confronted. I deny giving consent to a trip to the vending machines. I learn that I must make clear that a drink of water or a visit to the washroom is the limit of what they are allowed when they leave the room.

Again, I am reminded of how carefully and clearly teachers must express themselves, how they need to be guided by a knowledge of school regulations, and how there are students who try to get around them. Later, a senior teacher explains to me that students can go out of the room one or two at a time but they must sign out on a sheet near the door. In this way, if there is an incident in the building, administrators can check to see who was outside the classroom. This makes sense to me and I implement this rule.

There are other times when I allow a student to do something, and I have no idea I've violated school procedure. For example, we were asked to go to the gym so another class could take a test in our room. The students were not to play or exercise but had to sit on the benches. I was annoyed that they had nothing to do and were wasting their time. I gave my consent when a girl asked to listen to her Walkman. I didn't know that personal CD players are prohibited in school—yet all the students carry them. A few minutes later I watched my student get yelled at by the gym teacher. My student gave me a look, asking for support. I shrugged my shoulders, helpless, unsure of what to do. In my mind, listening to music made sense. For me as a new teacher, this was another painful example of what happens when you are unaware of accepted routines.

But it is equally painful for me to notice that wasting time is the norm. To sit there doing nothing is an invitation for a child to get into trouble, and it sends a message to kids that authority okays "hanging out." So much time is routinely wasted in school anyway—waiting in the hall, waiting for other kids to finish or quiet down, waiting for the teacher to get ready. Perhaps the issue of time for me is part of my own personal baggage. Starting over at age 40 made me want to live twice as fast in my new life. And because my own child nearly lost her life but was miraculously saved, I want to get the maximum out of every minute. I want to make the kids aware that their time in school counts, that what they do with their moments means something.

When I was an intern at the Louis Armstrong Middle School under Sid's supervision, he encouraged me to take the time to walk around, to observe, to get a feel for how teachers and students interact, and to gain an understanding of the school culture. The rhythms of the school amazed me. I could be standing in a quiet empty hallway and suddenly become engulfed with middle schoolers crowding the corridor and moving to other rooms. As quickly as they appeared, they disappeared. At I.S. 250 there isn't that kind of outburst. Many of the middle schoolers just move around the four "areas" of this room. Or perhaps because there is no bell, classes migrate from room to room. I don't often get the chance to observe how teachers move their classes from one room to another. I know that the practice in elementary schools is for children to line up by sex and size. Here, my adolescents, many of whom are too big for the chairs they sit on, rebel against walking quietly in anything that resembles a line. I ask them to get into two straight lines. Some shuffling of feet. "I'll wait," I say. One slinks behind another. They still talk. I follow at the rear. A veteran teacher from the high school stops my class and tells them they are the noisiest class he's ever heard and rude too. Didn't we know the high schoolers are taking a test? he asks and gives me a look as if to say, "Don't you know any better?" My students straighten up for a moment. But I'm the one who feels chastised.

Sid: Learning the Culture

One of the jobs for new teachers is to learn the habits, routines, and behaviors that reveal the beliefs, norms, and values of the school that have been built up over time. Maureen needs not only to absorb these aspects of school culture but to figure how to work with her classes in a way that minimizes conflict between what she believes and what the school demands.

At our Wednesday meeting I discuss with Maureen my experience working with teenagers at the Louis Armstrong Middle School when we talked about the school prohibition about wearing hats in the building. I told the students I had no objection to hats, but I was aware of the school rule and the ongoing battle to get conformity. I dealt with the problem openly. I pointed out that even though the wearing of hats didn't bother me, they would be reprimanded for doing so outside of class. We came to the conclusion that behavior appropriate in one situation may not be acceptable in other places. The use of curse words in the middle of a hotly contested basketball game is not a sin. In school, it is not all right to do so. A tank shirt suitable for a gym workout is not appropriate in English class.

I tell Maureen about walking into a classroom, when I was an elementary school principal, and asking the teacher why the children were allowed to chew gum. He replied, "I find that gum chewing relaxes the children, especially when they're taking tests." I leave satisfied with his response and with an understanding that others in the building may disagree and care will be taken regarding gum disposal.

An ongoing task in the mentorship is for me to help Maureen become conscious of her school's culture and the impact it has on her. I encourage her to be aware of the teachers around her, how they relate to each other and how she relates to them. We'll need to continue figuring out what we can do with the insights we identify.

Maureen: Spoken and Unspoken Rules

Following Sid's suggestion I continue observing my surroundings. At lunch I notice that the teachers' lounge is not unlike student lunchrooms, with cliques and private associations. I wonder who talks to whom and what they say. If you share something in confidence, does it end there? I see that teachers love to gossip. I'm concerned that if I express a feeling, there might be negative consequences.

A morning staff meeting focuses on the implementation of a new detention policy. For detention to work, the principal must depend on volunteers to remain after school. The staff, some grudgingly, agree to the plan. As I rush to pick up my own children at the end of the day, the need to find or extend my child care adds to my daily burden. I'm overwhelmed by all that is being asked of me. When the schedule is published, I notice that the name of another teacher, who also has children, is missing. I complain to a colleague, forgetting she's close to the teacher whose absence I've identified. She seems annoyed. I worry that I'll become the subject of angry discussion with her friend. Later, the teacher in question appears in my room. I watch her trying to gauge my intent: Was I really trying to get her in trouble or was I expressing my own anguish at being so overwhelmed? She says, "I've got to show you the ropes." This conversation reminds me that our principal is relying on volunteers and there's no reason I can't quietly say no. That in itself poses a challenge. But if one more person asks me to do something I'm going to lose it.

At this point I really appreciate that my mentor is not a member of the school staff. I know that what Sid and I discuss is private and that I can speak my mind freely. I never fear that he will say something negative about me to a colleague. Sometimes Sid pops in to see my principal, to say hello, to tell him how our relationship is progressing. I don't worry, as other first-year teachers do about their mentors, that Sid will report that my work is unsatisfactory. I appreciate the safe space our Wednesday meetings give me.

Sid: Other Teachers

It's Wednesday and we're talking in an empty classroom. A consultant from the district office opens the door to ask Maureen, who has skills in technology, to give assistance to a new computer teacher. She agrees to meet with him after school.

A few minutes later a colleague interrupts to get Maureen's okay for his class to join her group for a party. She assents, even though later she tells me that this teacher looks for ways to avoid work.

Maureen has also indicated to me that she agreed to write an article for a newspaper.

I watch with concern as Maureen consents to do all that is asked of her. I know how overwhelmed she is feeling lately. I want to help her to learn to say no. This is difficult for a new teacher who wants to get along with peers and be thought of as a contributor. But the energy drain for a beginning teacher is enormous, and Maureen has to guard her resources.

Sometimes I witness the insensitivity of other teachers. When Maureen gave a girl permission to listen to a Walkman in the gym and the physical education teacher, a veteran of the school, barked, "Get that thing out of your ear," I wanted to jump in, to let him know it's Maureen's role to deal with her children, and his interference diminishes her authority. I have seen the same thoughtlessness when administrators reprimand children for being noisy, as they pass through the halls, while their teacher seems a help-less bystander. I've also observed supervisors ignore the teacher's presence to discipline children in the middle of a lesson. I point out to Maureen that her role was subverted, and we consider how, when she is more sure of her-self, she can tell the teacher to make suggestions through her.

I remind Maureen to continue observing other teachers, to note how they interact with students and how they present content. She sees a teacher who rarely has a classroom management problem by always hav-ing the students involved in doing, working with their hands on a com-puter keyboard, playing with the art possibilities of a computer program, learning how to type. From a visit to another teacher, she recognizes that for children who have not learned to organize themselves, a predictable, well-planned environment is needed. She envies the easy manner of another colleague who uses a sense of humor to good advantage. In another classroom she finds someone who has mastery of management tricks. I indicate to Maureen that although there can be value in observing teachers who have particular strengths, there also can be unanticipated negative results. Instead of returning with useful ideas, the reaction might be feelings of inadequacy: Why can't I have clear routines like Miss B.? Why can't I let myself laugh like Mr. T.? Why can't I have better discipline like Miss I.?

My reservation about the value of learning to teach by watching others was supported by a former intern at the Louis Armstrong Middle School. In a final assessment of his internship he wrote:

> I have seen many good teachers over the past year. I admire Mr. D.'s enthusiasm, Mr. G.'s dedication, Ms. O.'s optimism, Ms. C.'s level-headedness, and Ms. B.'s flexibility. I spent my first 6 months of the year trying to decide which teacher had the most of these qualities so I could be like them when I am teaching. This frame of mind did more harm than good. While teaching is, in a way, a performing art, I am no longer trying to step into someone else's character when I am in front of the class. The hardest person to find when you are teaching is yourself. Because I was and am new to the profession, I felt the need to hide behind someone else's personality, because mine was too flawed, too inadequate to do the job on my own. No wonder I was a bundle of nerves.

My task is to help Maureen see that she need not be like anyone else and recognize her strengths. My job is to assist her in finding her own teaching voice.

I try to understand the pressures with which she has to deal, and I think back to when I started as a beginning teacher. I share with Maureen how I felt coming as a stranger to an environment I hadn't been in since I was an elementary school student. I tell her about how I, too, puzzled over where I belonged in the school community, and I know what it means when she says, "Even though I'm a teacher, I don't always feel like one." As a 24-year-old newcomer, part of me still felt like a child surrounded by grown-ups. When the teacher next door let out a shriek that penetrated to my room, I sensed myself inwardly jump as though I were the one being reprimanded. When I saw another veteran teacher whose soft voice disguised a will of steel gaining instant obedience from children, I heard an inner critical voice bemoaning my inability to get kids to react in the same way.

I let Maureen know that, like her, I looked to others for clues as to how to fit in, to take a class down a stairway in the approved manner, to allow students to go to the bathroom in accordance with school rules, or to have them use the correct school heading on test papers.

We talk about how natural discomfort is for anyone starting a new experience. A doctor doing his first operation, an actor beginning his career in theater, or a pilot flying his initial solo flight would all feel uncertainty about their ability to do the job.

I reassure Maureen that over time her confidence will grow and she will feel more at ease about dealing with others and the challenges that lie ahead. I urge her to seek out colleagues who can give assistance and support.

As Maureen's mentor, I recognize that for me to be effective I need constantly to refer back to my own beginnings as a teacher so that I can empathize with what she is experiencing. I don't ever want to forget how uncertain I felt, how much there was for me to learn, and how I wondered if I were cut out to be a teacher.

Maureen: In-House Support

Inspired by Sid's advice to get to know other teachers and observe them in action, I seek out RFK High School's assistant principal and English teacher, Nigel. He's a leader of RFK's peer coaching group, Critical Friends, and I want to be part of it even though I am reluctant to make yet another after-school commitment. While I don't join the Critical Friends group, Nigel agrees to do an intervisitation. It will serve a dual purpose: If he agrees to write up his observation of my class, it will be one less for my principal to do. I would benefit from a different point of view and an observation with a different protocol, and there is the added benefit that I can observe him.

Before I visit his class, he reviews observation protocol: what our goals are, what we will be looking for, and when we will meet afterwards to share what we noticed. He will be modeling "fishbowling" to show kids how to talk about their writing by engaging a small group of students in conversation in the center of the room while the rest of the class sits around the inner circle and observes quietly. Nigel has given me a purpose to my viewing: He wants me to kid watch, to see if they are indeed actively observing the fishbowl. He asks me to notice what the kids are doing while he participates in the fishbowl.

I had never seen a teacher fishbowl before, and it was something I immediately wanted to try. But I also had the chance to observe Nigel's tone with students, his classroom management style, his ease and comfort in front of the teenagers.

Nigel then came to observe me and my class. In our preobservation meeting I tell him I'm interested in teaching myself how to get kids to respond to each other on paper. I've been thinking through a way students would use a "double-entry journal," where they would put a quote from the text in the left column and write a response, reflection, or comment about that text in the right column. I was looking for a way that a second or possibly a third student could comment on the same piece of text. The logistics became complex, and Nigel listened as I thought out loud how I might accomplish this. Our goal for his observation was to see how this method worked.

In our postobservation conversation we reflected on how to fine-tune this method of written peer response. Nigel noted how long it had been since he observed 12- and 13-year-olds. He had forgotten how much they fidgeted. At first, he thought the boys fidgeted so much that they appeared not to be listening actively in class. On closer inspection though, he saw that they were indeed engaged in class conversation and their constant body movement was more an indication of their age than their involvement. The back-and-forth we had made me realize that there is an art, a skill, to classroom observation, and that often, to really understand what you are seeing, you need to understand the context in which the lesson is given.

When I see Sid on Wednesday, I'm going to tell him I took him up on his advice and share all that I learned.

CHAPTER 7

Job Pressures

Maureen: Will I Be Here Next Year?

As I begin to enjoy a sense of belonging, my principal informs me that my job is a one-year appointment. Perhaps this was a reminder; in the whirlwind of my hiring a lot was said to me that I did not remember. I will have to reapply for my job if I want to stay. At first I am chagrined. All I can think about is being considered again, that under-the-microscope feeling of being interviewed by a panel of parents and teachers, worrying about my competition, who else might apply—with stronger qualifications or more seniority. I do not realize how lucky I am: that I can reinterview because my school participates in a "school-based option," meaning that the majority of the staff has voted to depart from standard operating procedures.

In most schools in New York City the United Federation of Teachers mandates rules of seniority, and there are teachers asking for transfers to my district. Had I been at a school that didn't govern itself by a school-based option plan, I would not know what school I would work in or what grade. One teacher tells me it took her 10 years of teaching before she was able to settle in one school and grade.

Despite whispers from my colleagues not to worry, I worry. I carry my family's health insurance because my husband is a freelance writer. The thought of not having medical coverage frightens me because I have a child who requires special medication. And, like a typical teacher, I'm not a person who appreciates change.

When I gather my thoughts and become a little more rational, I feel sad that I might not be able to teach the curriculum I've been planning and rehearsing all year. I have also been gathering books for those units of study. I don't want to repeat my first year with all its stresses and unknowns. I don't have it in me to live this year all over again. Not now anyway. I feel exhausted, bewildered, and in light of this dubious employment news, depressed. While my students are at lunch, I sit at my desk, stare straight out into space, leaning my head in my hands.

My principal, on one of his frequent rounds of the building, spots me like this.

"What's wrong?" he asks.

I confide, "Reapplying for my job has got me down."

He doesn't respond directly, but conveys his understanding and returns to his rounds.

The next Wednesday I communicate my worries to Sid. He encourages me to set them aside. "You're a vital member of the group," he said. "They'd be silly to let you go." And then, "I'll go speak to your principal and see what I can learn."

I try to let his words transform my negative thinking. They don't.

Sid: Dealing with Maureen's Worry

From the look on Maureen's face I can tell it's one of those days. She tells me about having to reinterview for her job and of her worry. As we move to her empty classroom to talk, I feel pressure to say something, to do something to alleviate her concerns. After offering Maureen rational responses about her value to the school, I assure her that I will talk to the principal. I realize how important it is that I have established a relationship with him, and I am confident he will give weight to what I say. I tell her that at one of our meetings we'll discuss how to deal with student testing. I stress the idea that she needs to develop balance in her life and recognize that there are limits to what she can do.

My response seems weak. I wonder if anything I've said has relieved the pressure she feels. What can I do that is helpful? I listen. But the value of attending closely is useful only to the extent of the trust and comfort Maureen feels as she tells of her concerns. I think about our meetings in which we don't only discuss pedagogy, classroom events, adolescent characteristics, and other school matters. We also talk about the books we've been reading, how her children are doing in school, her graduate coursework, and her poetry writing. I tell her about my son and daughter and my attempts to inculcate them as lovers of books. I express my concerns about my involvement in the development of a campus school and my own frustrations as a beginning teacher. By holding a mirror to each other's experiences we give up our privacy for openness of expression.

The fact remains, however, that the sense of being overwhelmed is a condition new teachers inevitably face.

Maureen: Observation Worry

My principal schedules a time to observe me. This is something I dread even though I now know my principal is kindhearted. But with having to reapply for my job, I feel pressure to really perform. This observation is not the same as when Sid sits in the back of the room or even when Nigel visited. They are in my room with the purpose of helping me grow as a teacher, not to rate or grade me. This particular observation is a test and not a learning experience. And with this test comes all the usual fright.

The preobservation meeting is brief and does not resemble at all the Critical Friends protocol I followed with Nigel. Supervisors, I learn, do not generally implement that protocol. I ask fellow teachers in other schools and they relate horror stories about their observations, lacking any pre- or postobservation conversation. Principals select times to observe that are good for them and not the teacher. Others tell me that the observations are an opportunity for a principal who doesn't like you to formalize that in writing and make it difficult for you to remain in the school. On the other hand, a new teacher I know praised her principal: "She came in and saw I was having a difficult day and whispered she would come back at a better time."

From my area it is easy for the principal to observe me at any time on his rounds of the building—and he does. But the formality of the observation adds pressure. I quiz my colleagues about what it will be like. Is he a harsh critic? Does he make recommendations to you afterwards? Is he critical by nature? Does he offer readings on teaching methods?

He will come to see the eighth graders Sid observed earlier in the year. Partly because of their discussion about bullies and victims and feelings of outsiderness, I selected the biography *Across America on an Emigrant Train* (1993) by Jim Murphy for them to read together. It is about the writer Robert Louis Stevenson, who traveled from Scotland to California in the 1880s to marry the love of his life, a woman named Fanny—who happened to already be married. Not only does the book give us an understanding of that historical period, it demonstrates the power, not the impotence, of being an outsider.

My students came to the story with emotional understanding and so could connect sensitively and deeply to the reading. (Of course, they were also horrified that Stevenson made this trip without the benefit of cash machines or a cellular phone.) When a repairman worked on our classroom's heater while this class was in session, he noted the enthusiastic participation and conversation. He turned to us and asked, "Is this a gifted class?" I shook my head and said "no," but I regretted that "no" from the moment it flew out of my mouth. A *certainly* or a *yes* would have made my young scholars feel appreciated. I told myself I had to compliment that group more; they deserved it.

This class was equally stellar on the day that our principal visited. When he left the class quietly, we had no immediate validation. My students asked, "Were we okay? Do you think he liked what he saw?"

"Definitely," I said. "You were wonderful."

Sid: Principals

Maureen tells me the observation went well. The students participated actively. They behaved and they seemed interested in the story. She believes she'll get a good report but adds, "I'm not sure where it all leads."

She goes on to say, "I think I'm feeling less uncomfortable about having someone observing in my room, and our previous talks about leading group discussions helped."

I'm gratified to hear that what we've been doing together has had some payoff. Just as Maureen needs to feel she's growing, it helps for me to hear that we've been making progress.

When I ask Maureen about her principal, she says, "He doesn't micromanage the staff. He gives us lots of freedom to choose what we teach and how we teach." Her principal is creative and without hesitation would paint a mural alongside a group of youngsters. He tries to supply teachers with materials for creative learning to whatever extent possible. On top of everything, he works without an assistant principal and is occupied doing many things.

I remember my principal, when I was a teacher, as a distant figure who was bogged down with parents, the community, and the district office and had little time to consider how I was doing in the classroom. He left me alone and I felt alone struggling to master routines, to find ways to keep children interested, to learn about the best approaches to teaching different areas of the curriculum, and to feel good about what I was doing. How I would have welcomed words of encouragement, someone to hear my frustrations, to offer ideas, and to be there as I learned to teach. I hope I fill that role for Maureen.

I think of principals and the influence they have on new teachers like Maureen. Some are dedicated to the appearances of teaching. These are supervisors who upon entering a room note if the lesson aim on the blackboard and if the bulletin board displays refer to specific standards. They check to see if the teacher is following the schedule written in her plan book and if books are neatly arranged on shelves. There are other administrators who are warm and empathic and function in a way respectful of the teacher's authority. But no matter what their leadership style, all principals hold positions of power, and their support is preferable to their harassment. In some situations a new teacher gets "on the bad side" of a principal, and then she may find herself assigned an undesirable schedule, subject to constant criticism, and made to feel unappreciated.

I point out to Maureen that just as she is learning to "read" children, she also needs to learn to "read" administrators and to establish her worth to the school. I suggest that rather than waiting to have contact with her principal, it would be worthwhile to be proactive, sending him samples of her students' work, inviting him to class to see a pupil presentation, sharing with him her reaction to a book or an article she's read.

When I meet with Maureen's principal, since her ability has been in evidence, I am able to fortify a reputation she has already created for herself. But from other mentors I hear about problems they encounter in talks with administrators about the progress of their mentees. There are instances in which the school head complains about a new teacher's weakness and wonders why the mentor has not succeeded in improving matters. In other cases the principal asks that the mentor make certain that the mentee follow the teaching methodology prescribed by the district office.

I consider how I would respond. In each situation I would ask about the problems that have been identified and the ways in which school personnel have tried to deal with them. I would seek suggestions as to how I, as mentor, could fit into a school-based plan to assist the new teacher. As I inquire, I would avoid any inclination to place myself in the role of savior, the solver of all problems. Instead, I would attempt to arrange for a three-way meeting in which the principal, my mentee, and I could set up goals and decide on approaches to providing assistance. I would continue helping my mentee by making suggestions, providing material, asking questions, guiding her to resources, supporting, encouraging, listening, and all the while keeping her principal informed so that my efforts are part of a schoolwide approach to teacher improvement.

As I try to be clearer about Maureen's relationship with her principal and about how administrators operate today, I go back to the time when I was head of an elementary school in Harlem. Whenever I explore the past, I catch myself painting an idealized picture of how I functioned, something supervisors and mentors are prone to do. The farther I'm away from my days as school leader, the more perfect I think things were. I forget the times I made the wrong decision, the burden of responsibility I carried with me always. I block out the crazy aftermath of the teachers' strike with parents and professionals at each other's throats, the nights I came home to vent to my wife, "There's no way to get through to them. It's like everyone is deaf." I don't dwell on the awful sense of aloneness I felt at the end of a school day, when I'd sit at my desk trying to collect myself. I relished the quiet, but how I wished there were others with whom I could share my worries, my concerns, my ideas.

And yet I tried to be for the school staff what I want to be for Maureen; a mentor, someone who nurtures, guides, stimulates. Each morning and afternoon I walked the building—to reassure a beginner that she could succeed despite the difficulties she's facing, to share an article I had read with another, to invite teachers to come with me to a professional conference, and to confer with others about particular children. I worked with teachers in classrooms to start individualized reading programs. I arranged for consultants from Bank Street College of Education and student teachers from Queens College to support instruction. I went beyond the City University to find graduates of colleges like Harvard, Yale, and Washington University eager to work in an inner-city neighborhood and be given freedom and encouragement to try different approaches. I led parents and teachers in the battle to get the Board of Education to build a new wing to the building to accommodate overcrowding.

But like Maureen, I had moments of discouragement. A newly appointed teacher turns down an assignment to our school because her parents are fearful of her working in Harlem. A parent meeting draws only a handful of parents. A fire in a nearby building uproots the families of children attending our school. District office demands for observation reports, safety plans, attendance data, budget figures, and more descend upon the school. But each day I returned to work with staff.

My memories make me loathe to criticize for I know how overwhelming the job of principal can be and I see how crucial it is for administrators, pulled as they are in different directions, to have the help of mentors to work with beginning teachers.

CHAPTER 8

Relating to Parents

Maureen: Seeking Advice on Parents

I want Sid to advise me on how to handle parent meetings. It's an enormous task to convey a total picture of each student's performance in a meeting that lasts only minutes. The time allotted is just enough for all parties to meet. To keep the teachers in my school on schedule our principal bought us digital timers. Other teachers use student monitors to direct traffic and maintain the flow of parents in and out of the room.

I'm still in shock over the experience I had with the "drive-through" conferences this fall. Before those meetings I dreamt about them. In one dream I was initiating a conference and then found myself struggling midway through the session. Throughout the day, whether I was in the shower or spreading peanut butter for my children's lunch sandwiches, I'd rehearse what I was going to say to the different parents. Other teachers showed me how to create notes on students on a bank of index cards. They didn't seem to help. I worried that I would unceremoniously blurt out that a kid never shuts up. I worried that I'd freeze on the spot and forget the specifics of what I wanted to communicate to the parent. I worried about how my words to parents would translate back to the middle schoolers at home. I remembered myself as a student waiting up nervously for my mother to return and tell me what the teacher had said.

At lunchtime before the scheduled conferences two teachers did a skit. One played the role of a parent and the other a teacher. One teacher spoke in "educational-ese" and the other translated her words into plain English. We rolled with laughter. For me, and probably the others, this served as a release of tension as we planned out what we were going to say, how we were going to say it, and fussed with displays of student work in our rooms.

At the fall conferences I was surprised by what I observed. Many parents were just holding things together and admitted utter powerlessness over their children. Others asserted that getting the child to do homework was the teacher's responsibility. There were also those who shared the hurt of a divorce and apologized for the child's acting out.

As a parent, perhaps I too tried to explain why my daughter cried so much and give reasons for her behavior in the classroom. As a teacher, though, I didn't attempt to understand why a child was acting the way he did. I wanted to convey information quickly and identify ways to enhance the student's performance. Maybe that was an error.

My inexperience showed when I offered an assessment to a boy's father in too blunt a fashion. "Your son needs to work on sentence structure and spelling. He also needs to concentrate better, to focus on material, and not let himself be distracted." The father, after a moment's hesitation, came back at me, "Not one of his teachers ever told me that before."

"Well, maybe these problems are just coming up," I replied, trying to be as delicate as I could. As I spoke to the parent, I thought that he was in denial about his son's weaknesses. The boy's record was filled with low standardized scores and mediocre grades. Only afterwards did I realize that my bluntness may have caused him to be defensive. Still, it bewilders me how—despite my inelegant phrasing—a parent would challenge my professional assessment and recommendation.

Other parents brought their children with them—which surprised me. When I saw a parent with a student, I included the youngster in our discussion. I made a note to myself to learn more about how to have students participate in parent-teacher conferences.

As the meetings continued, I heard some parents threaten to use physical force on their children if they didn't "shape up." I saw parents who themselves had not had a good school experience and felt intimidated by their children's homework. Parents who were nonreaders challenged me: "What's the big deal if my kid doesn't read at home?" They shrugged off the new state requirement that children read 25 books a year. I encountered parents who were disappointed in their lives and saw their children following in their footsteps. They regarded this passively, as if no amount of parental strength could overcome fate or genetics or society. Driving home drained, I reviewed these conversations in my head. An endless stream of alternating voices, my own self-critical self spliced in for heightened effect. If only I could have just reinforced the idea that for kids to succeed in school they need a home life that gives that success number one priority—whether it's a calm place to do homework, nourishing meals, unstructured "hang out" time with parents, or enough sleep. But I'm sure none of that came to the table. It takes me hours to unwind and afterwards I have a restless slumber. When I see Sid on Wednesday, I say, "Remember when we spoke about effective parent-teacher conferences?"

He remembers.

"Can we spend some more time discussing how to relate to parents?"

"Of course." As I tell him about my experience, he listens intently and takes notes to remind him of what I am saying and what he will want to pursue at length and in depth.

Sid: Exploring Ways to Work with Parents

At most middle schools I hear little of parents coming to teachers to discuss the progress of their children. Even during Open School Week, attendance at scheduled parent-teacher conferences is minimal. It's as though in the middle school years, in contrast to the elementary grades, parents have bought into the myth that adolescents, in their desire for independence, want mothers and fathers to stay distant from their school lives. But the fact is that their sons and daughters continue to crave the recognition and support of their parents, who remain a primary influence.

Despite the limited contact, Maureen, like all teachers, has concerns about how to deal with parents in a productive manner. Everywhere the message is heard: "Parent involvement is essential to student growth." Their role increases in importance as they are mandated to be the majority group on School Leadership teams and on panels to choose school personnel. They have become active participants in groups evaluating educational programs.

Maureen wants parents to work with her, but she worries about how to involve them. She describes her concerns:

"What do I say? What do I do? My principal warns us to be wary about what we communicate to parents. He explains that we're just a phone call away from becoming a newspaper headline."

She tells me about an experienced teacher who encountered trouble because in reprimanding a child for misbehavior she used the word *depressed*. The term raised a red flag for the parent, ever sensitive to criticism of her daughter. She challenged the teacher, "Who are you to label my daughter depressed? Are you a psychiatrist?"

Maureen notes in her log, "Even the most seasoned pro can get entangled with a difficult parent. How careful you need to be about what you say to a child or parent!"

She goes on to say, "I have every kind of parent, from those who care a lot to those who never come to school. I have articulate parents and those who can't speak English. I have disorganized, inept parents and those who are a tremendous support for their kids."

I try to understand what it means for Maureen having to deal with so much parent diversity and with the increased scrutiny of every teacher action or word. I pause to look back on my life as teacher and parent. As a novice in my early twenties faced with parents who had raised children, I felt intimidated by the sense that I was deemed the expert prepared to answer any and all questions about child development and learning. It was a role I was ill-equipped to fill. I have since learned that my job is not just to give solutions but to join with the parent in looking at problems together.

My experience with parents was different from what teachers now face: No more coffee and cake PTAs for parents now, but rather, inclusion on School Leadership Teams to approve curriculum, to make decisions about budget, and to evaluate teachers. In the middle-class neighborhood in which I taught, parents were reluctant to question let alone attack, teachers and the school. At Christmas I was smothered with gifts of aftershave lotion and ties rather than suspicious queries about my teaching methods.

Ideas on how to work with parents emerge from our discussions. I suggest to Maureen that, with parent sessions so tightly scheduled the night of the "drive-through conferences," it makes sense to limit goals. For those children about whom she has concerns, it would be better to arrange a parent meeting when more time is available. For others, establishing a relationship and identifying ways to work together might be all that can be expected in the brief time available.

Maureen realizes how important it is to keep parents informed. "I use e-mail and the telephone a lot," she says, "and would like to be able to send a newsletter home telling parents what the youngsters are doing in class."

We also talk about writing letters to parents. I caution Maureen about how open to misinterpretation words on paper can be. I advise: "If possible, the goal is to talk to parents in person. It's only then that real exchange happens. Use letters to arrange personal contact rather than putting anything substantive in writing."

Maureen tells me abut parents who themselves experienced schools as places of failure, about parents whose family life is in disarray, about parents with unrealistic expectations for their children, and about parents whose cultural values are out of sync with those of the school.

I remind Maureen of how the aim of a parent-teacher conference is to initiate a cooperative relationship, which means that the time together will not simply be used to list student deficiency but rather will communicate a valuing of the child's strengths and an examination of ways to make the school year most productive. The teacher's ability to listen, to communicate interest, and to establish a welcoming atmosphere increases the likelihood of ongoing contact.

Together we develop a list of suggestions about how to conduct a conference:

- Avoid sitting behind the teacher's desk.
- Include the child when appropriate.
- Have student work readily accessible.
- Seek the parent's input into analysis of problems.
- Acknowledge parent's feelings and listen closely to what they have to say.
- Ask the parent if he or she has any questions.
- Finish with a summary of cooperatively identified conclusions and future plans.
- Arrange for follow-up contact.

But working effectively with parents demands going beyond a mechanical following of suggested steps. It calls for empathy, careful listening, and an ability to connect with others.

Sid and Maureen: The Angry Parent

It's Wednesday and I am to meet with Maureen at her room. As I approach Maureen's class I hear a parent's angry words: "I didn't keep her home for no good reason. I called the office to tell them she had to see the dentist." She ignores Maureen's concern about the girl's frequent absence. This is a natural lead-in for our topic today.

We had decided to try taping our sessions not only to record our conversations and the ways we cover topics, but to examine the way a mentor and mentee relate to each other. What follows is a transcript of excerpts from our discussion.

Sid: Did she just come in on her own?

Maureen: No, I left a message on her answering machine. Every time her class has a test first period, Jane is either late or absent. This absence was an in-your-face I'm not taking your test. I got angry. I called.

Jane had been held over last year, and her test scores are low, and there are all the times she misses school. I'm stumped about how to get her mother involved, to have her stay involved, and to see things my way. I have quite a few parents whose kids are failing, and I call the parents. I don't want to sound like I'm telling on the kids, but I guess it does sound like that. I feel we need to train the parents to get on the ball and work with their kids.

Sid: The question that comes to my mind is what is the purpose of meeting with parents. You stated one goal when you said you want them to be involved. You go on to suggest that you're not going to get them involved if you just give them a list of accusations. When you repeat, "This is what your kid is doing bad," the parent's likely, unspoken reaction is "I feel guilty." The question then is how to get her involved so that she doesn't feel attacked but sees she has a constructive role to fill.

One of the ways I would think about this is to consider how I would feel when a teacher calls and fires away with a report of my child's failings. I'd rather hear that I have something to offer, that there's something I can do. I would also want to hear that my child has value.

Maureen (deep sigh): I don't know. Yesterday one of the teachers phoned a parent and asked her to take her child to the library. The parent said, "I don't have time to do that." This made the teacher angry, and she replied, "What do you mean you don't have time to take your child to the library? We take the children to the school library all the time. But we need support from the home."

Sid: It seems to me that in this instance the parent needs support too. Suppose the teacher had said, "I know you're interested in your child reading books and I realize you are very busy. You work and have lots to do. But could we talk about ways to get more books into the hands of your child?" It turns the tone around. If the teacher gets angry, the parent gets defensive. There is a reality to what the parent says. She works hard, she gets tired. She may have her own personal problems. But if you give credit for caring about her kid's reading and try to get her working on the problem with you, you may succeed in getting her involved. You don't get her involved by attacking her inability to do something. You get her involved by acknowledging and supporting her interest in her child.

In the case of Jane's mother I wonder what her reaction would be if you had said, "I know Jane's health is important to you and that it is difficult to get a dentist's appointment. But is there something we can do together to help Jane achieve better in school?"

Maureen: What if you've reached a high-pressure zone with the kids? I had four parent meetings last week. One of my girls was dating a high school boy. She's a smart girl, but her grades were plummeting. The mother, who is a teacher, met with me and acknowledged that it was her fault.

Sid: She blames herself?

Maureen: Yes. Why? She has several kids with different fathers, and she finally remarried. The new husband, after only a short time, left. And that's when my student started taking up with this boy and her grades took a nosedive. We had a sad, difficult meeting, but the mother supported our decision to curb her daughter's frequent visits to the bathroom—occasions to meet her boyfriend. Since the meeting I've seen a tiny bit of improvement. Still, I'm not sure it made any real difference. When we ask a parent to change something, we're really asking for a lifestyle change. If you have a child who's always disorganized and then you meet the mother who is totally disorganized, you're not going to get results unless the mother learns to organize herself.

Time and time again I see how hard it is to get and sustain parent support. An example: I have a child who never does any homework. His mother became very angry at the teachers because we wanted to have him evaluated [for possible learning disabilities]. She promised that he's going to do his homework. He did a couple of assignments, and now he's not doing his homework again. What am I supposed to do—keep badgering the mother to get after her son?

Sid: I realize that maintaining communication with parents takes a lot of physical and emotional energy. Making telephone calls the way you do and using e-mail can be enormously helpful. But we come back to what we said at the beginning. Our purpose in talking to parents is to involve them in solving problems and stimulating kids to do the best they can.

Suppose with the homework issue you had started by saying to the parent, "Ms. Jones, I'm concerned that Johnny doesn't do his homework. Do you have any ideas why?" Immediately I want to bring her into the picture. In a sense she's a better expert than you are. She knows the kid. She lives with him. So you ask, "Are there things we can do together so that Johnny can be regular about his homework?" She may or may not have ideas. You ask, "Is there a special place in your apartment that can be given over to where he can keep his books and do his homework? Do you think there could be a regular time right before supper or right after, before the TV goes on, when homework could be done? Is there some way you and I could follow up in case he's forgetful?"

A discussion of that sort communicates the idea that you're working together. It may work or it may not. If it works, great. At the end of the week you write the parent a note. "I just want to tell you that our discussions have proved very helpful. Johnny's been doing his homework." Or if it doesn't work, you share ideas about what else to do. I know this takes a lot of psychic energy. But does it sound at all reasonable?

Maureen: It sounds reasonable—at the beginning of the year when everyone is hopeful and optimistic and willing.

Sid: I know. I know—and then you run out of energy.

Maureen: Yes, you run out of energy, and you get angry.

Sid: And you feel defeated. It's not working.

Maureen: I do feel defeated sometimes. Even if I get a parent who asks for a list of homework assignments so that her child may catch up, I'm not always able to supply it. I scribble the assignments in my book and forget what date I assigned what. That's the importance of keeping scrupulously organized. Sometimes I'm not.

Sid: Problems don't have single, final solutions. That's true of homework and other issues as well. In regard to homework there are a number of things to consider: Are we dealing with a disorganized home life? Is the homework meaningful? Am I consistent about how I follow up on homework assignments? Do I integrate homework into classroom work? Do I keep parents informed about the place of homework in the curriculum? But always you do what you can to involve parents meaningfully in working with you to help the child.

Maureen: Listening to Myself

When I go back and listen to the tape we made, I become aware of two things. The first is that I am not a good listener. I cut Sid off. I interject things. I resist his ideas and what he has to say. My head is swirling in defensiveness, which I admit to with only the tape recorder as my witness. I examine the nature of my defensiveness: I've done all I can and it's not enough, and I've got to learn and modify and adapt.

Even though I'm a first-year teacher, I find myself with the mental stance of defensive veteran teachers in other schools. To them, the reason why they don't succeed as teachers is because of the kids. "It's the kid's fault." "The kids don't want to learn." "The parents don't make learning a priority in the home." "Parents don't support teachers. They demean them at home and the kids come to school with their parents' attitudes."

To a certain extent I've created my own difficulties by being so emotional—and so ambitious. Had I taken a calmer, mellower tone, I probably would have achieved more in my conferences with parents. But right now listening to Sid's thoughtful suggestions just make me feel more drained and exhausted. I get angry at the parents who don't, won't, or can't control their children. I'm outraged that these children roam aimlessly in the afternoons and are allowed out so late. All kids need to be in specific places, doing specific things, and must be accountable, in the after-school hours, especially, to their parents. Many are not. And those children come to school unprepared and become disruptive.

I close my eyes as I listen to Sid's voice advocating for understanding and not anger. Between the lines of his dialogue I hear him ask me to be teacher to both parent and child. I must partner with parents so that they too can guide their children toward success. And I also realize that what students report back to their parents about what I say or do in the classroom is influenced by the parent-student relationship.

I understand that my success depends on my skills as a motivator and as a communicator of expectations. I must work smarter, not harder. Make better choices. Rather than confronting issues head-on, I might be better off using a warmer, calmer tone to have parents better understand what we can do together to serve the child's best interests. I realize too that I'm harsh on myself and that my growth as a teacher and a skillful communicator with parents will come through a series of small steps. As I anticipate my next parent meeting, I know I'm not there to scold the parents but to get their views of the problem and attempt a baby step with them. I'm not going to go into the meeting thinking about 12 things, wanting to tell the parent all 12. I'm going to zoom in on just one thing at a time.

Still, even listening to myself think out loud about this, I must acknowledge that some part of me has grown sharply cynical. And it's no use to ignore it.

Sid: Reacting to Maureen's Reaction

When I hear Maureen's frustration, I wonder if I've said too much, too fast. I ask myself if I call for too much understanding as she faces some parents who "don't, won't, or can't control their children." Do I look for perfection in a context of too little teacher support and dysfunctional family life? And yet my optimistic nature continues to advocate searching for ways to reach past the walls of the school to invite fathers and mothers to join in educating their children. I realize also there are moments in a teacher's life when cynicism outweighs hope. But I know in Maureen's case these are temporary dips and not the essence of who she is.

I am also concerned that my suggestions to Maureen come from a view distorted by my own experience, which no longer mirrors the reality of schools. Although I continually return to my time as student, new teacher, veteran instructor, and administrator to help me identify with Maureen and her school culture, I recognize that to help a new teacher I need to be clear about the extent to which my school past does or does not relate to the present. I remember visiting the high school I attended.

I came to a world different from the one I knew—security guards, metal detectors, student identification cards, and graffiti-marked walls. I was stamped by a different educational environment.

I also have to remind myself that the task of working with parents has grown more complicated than when I was a teacher. Today it is more common for both parents to be working with the result that they are more difficult to reach. Single-parent homes are more prevalent. Language differences are a more frequent factor in discussions about the students we teach.

Maureen and I talk about how recent decades have seen schools take on duties previously assumed by parents—breakfasts, lunches, after-school supervision, and, most important, time for adults and youngsters to share feelings and thoughts. More and more students enter the school on Monday mornings with emotional burdens that remain unexplored. But here again we think about these societal dynamics, not to allow parents and communities to abdicate responsibility, but to understand the difficulties facing families and schools.

Our discussions take us beyond a focus on the skills of conferencing with parents to a consideration of how to include them in their youngsters' education. The "drive-through" parent-teacher conferences and the periodic distribution of report cards not only do an inadequate job of providing information about students but do little to involve their most significant teachers—the parents—in their education.

Maureen and I consider what can be done. We recall how, at the Louis Armstrong Middle School where Maureen served as an intern, an annual parent-teacher retreat was held in which accomplishments were shared, goals were set, and cooperative activities were planned. The parents were also invited to participate in a parent-student day in which adults followed their youngsters through their normal school day schedule.

I share with her ideas and material I've picked up at other schools. In one place, the teacher sent home family assignments such as asking the parents to contribute artifacts and photographs for a class study of different cultures. In another instance, a group researching wrestling as a sport not as an exhibition solicited articles and on-line information from parents and succeeded in having one boy's uncle, who participated in the sport at college, to come to the class. In another class, the teacher surveyed the parents to identify hobbies, backgrounds, and interests so that they could be invited as resource people to contribute to the curriculum exploration. I also tell her about schools where parent-student book clubs have been established in which adult and youngsters read the same book. Activities such as these give a different definition to the traditional teacher-parent relationship. It becomes one that is cooperative rather than adversarial.

With her interest in and knowledge of technology, Maureen suggests setting up a website on which homework and special activities of the class can be listed. E-mail messages giving reminders and announcing holiday happenings for parents and students can become a regular feature of school operation.

We agree to continue exploring ways of making parents participants in their youngsters' education rather than viewing them as passive receivers of information.

CHAPTER 9

The Standardized Test

Maureen: Thinking About Tests

From my log:

It's April and here are just a few adjectives about the way I feel at 8:25 A.M. Harried. Scattered. Frazzled. I have a stiff neck. I'm worried about my hair. My skin. How I look. Every time I started to do something last night to prepare for my teaching day, one of my children called. Elizabeth, my eight-year-old, is totally unwrapped because she was having her standardized math test this morning and her teacher told the class that this test could mean summer school or repeating the grade. Elizabeth is excellent at math. At the dinner table she said, "I am confident about the reading test because I know if I just read the questions carefully I'll do all right. But this is the math test! I'm not good at math." I tell her that she's very good in math, as her report card indicates. But the fact is that she isn't the fastest math thinker around. Other children in her class get the concepts more quickly. I have always been angry that these tests are timed. Are they measuring how much a child knows, how they can withstand the pressure of being timed, or just how fast they can perform the math?

My child's worry at home makes me sympathize with what my students experience. I never thought that standardized test scores reflected what I truly knew. It is only now, because I've taken so many tests for my certification, that I can perform well on these exams. In test-taking preparation courses I learned strategies highlighting the need to "think like the test writer," to understand the concept of "the best answer," which might not necessarily be the one I would give. I've come to believe that to excel on standardized tests you've got to turn off part of yourself, the part that wants to be creative. Taking a test is not about being an individual. It's about being able to accommodate to the test writer's agenda. One of my instructors offered this counsel for taking the state teacher exam: "Imagine yourself the perfect teacher in a rural community. That's what they are looking for." He went on to advise, "When writing an essay, it doesn't matter what you believe in as long as you articulate the position carefully."

I've been coaching my students too. When we examine multiple-choice questions, I recommend that my students eliminate what is definitely incorrect and wrestle with the final two possibilities. For essays, I warn them not to spend a lot of time thinking about original ideas. I tell them that they can write notes in the test booklet. They've got to unlearn what we've been doing all year: brainstorming, drafting, revising, developing their thinking over time. Now they have to produce an essay in one draft within a time limit. It doesn't seem right.

Test days bring test daze. The number of tests is too difficult to comprehend. As they roll in, I see some students shut off while others become numb. Those who have done little all year do even less. The more able pupils freeze with anxiety. All feel overwhelmed with just how many two-day tests they will have to experience. I wondered how to keep the worried balanced and the nonfunctioning performing.

I also think about how I'm working during this marathon of test taking. In the politically charged atmosphere of teacher salaries debates and merit pay schemes, I feel blotted out, no energy to burn. I wonder if it's worth it. Our school's test grades will be reported in the newspaper, numbers in black and white that demean and malign the urban teacher. I question whether it makes sense to continue prodding students to produce and to be fearful of being held over should they not score well on the test. I need a better incentive for the kids to attend after-school test prep sessions. I don't feel compensated adequately for the angst, extra hours, and time necessary to e-mail parents. It no longer makes sense to keep pushing, cajoling, and lecturing my students on the consequences of low test scores.

Sid is anxious to hear about the tests and how I'm responding to them. My response is somewhat evident: I look harried, nearly unkempt. I feel that my success or failure as a teacher rests on how my students score. While Sid does not come out and say so, I know his back is up at all these tests. When we meet, he tries to place all this testing within a context. "Test scores do not define your success or failure as a teacher," he tells me. "It's the teaching you do all year. Think of the test as another spring ritual." He gives me a copy of an article he's authored, "My Life With Tests," (2000) and I slip it between the sheets of a binder to read later.

I have never felt myself to be a successful test taker. I have stinging memories of debating between those two nearly right answers before making an arbitrary decision about which one to bubble in. Right now this testing is testing me in what I already know, and that's what I must rely on. I think about what would have helped me as a student (and was never done) or what might help my daughter (and is not done), and I try to give my students some of that. Sid does some research and brings books to me to read, but knowing how burdened I am with work, he chunks out what's important and targets specific questions for me to read. Certainly, test taking is becoming its own genre, its own lengthy course of study, which I can see should be incorporated into every teacher's training.

This is the first year that my eighth graders will be taking a new state-administered test in English Language Arts. It is a standards-based test, and so its tasks should reflect curriculum in those classrooms adhering to new state-issued guidelines, which aim to achieve new, vigorous educational parameters. The test begins with the familiar "bubble in" timed format assessing students' reading comprehension. Afterwards, on this day, is a listening section. Students are asked to listen to a selection read to them twice by their teacher and take notes, fill out a "T" chart and write a response and an extended response. On the second day students are asked to read lengthy passages and respond to what they've read in writing. There too they write short and extended responses. The second day of the test also includes an independent writing assignment that is usually, but not always, thematically related to the reading portion.

A week before my eighth graders take their English Language Arts (ELA) exam, one final detail occurs to me: Breakfast. They don't eat it—even it if is available to them in school before classes start. They are usually starved and can't concentrate during the period before lunch, just when I figure they will be engaged in the most demanding portion of the test. I decide to make sure they get a morning meal. My principal permits me to request funds from the PTA. I purchase fresh bagels, cream cheese, and orange juice. Another teacher brings her eighth-grade class to my room so that they too can eat breakfast. Food disappears. The adolescents who told me that they weren't hungry are suddenly ravenous. Later, I am pleased as I observe my students taking their ELA and writing with energy.

The next day I received a letter from a parent.

Dear Mrs. Robins,
Andrew told me you brought in bagels and cream cheese for all of them in the class so they would have a full stomach before the test. I think that was one of the nicest things I've heard. I must tell you that

you are truly an exceptional person. I knew you were special before, now I'm sure of it.

Wow. That made me feel good. It's what politicians don't understand. A letter like that is merit pay.

Sid: Dealing with Tests

This Wednesday's meeting occurs in the middle of test-taking time. Maureen talks to me about a school fixated on test scores. Maureen tells me, "It's all around me, it is constant, it never lets up. Tests, tests, tests. The kids are swamped. Tests in social studies, science, math, English, technology, Spanish, earth science. We're dealing with numbers, not learning."

She vents her concerns. "There's this push to cover material that might be on the test. Everything is about getting ready for the test. In a nearby school for a whole month they did nothing but test preparation. They even hired a consultant to help them. I've gotten the message loud and clear that I'm to do whatever I can to improve test results."

She describes her worries about the students. "The kids think the end of the year is when they finish the tests, and the less able students shut down, begin to act out."

She goes on to express anger about what is happening. "This craze for better examination numbers is chipping away at any sense of professionalism I might have. Decisions about promotion and holding children back are made on the basis of a mark on one test. What I've learned about a child over an entire year counts for very little. I wonder if the test makers know anything about schools and children."

When I listen to Maureen's worries, when I read reports of New York City teachers not wanting to teach the fourth grade because high-stakes tests are given at that level, and when I hear the pronouncements of politicians, I feel frustration about the testing madness that has taken over the entire country.

My concern grows when I see that the general public cannot think of schools without thinking about standardized tests, and that automatic connection makes for a high level of student anxiety. As Maureen indicates in her log, her daughter worries that she will not get a high enough grade to be admitted to a special class. My niece tells me, "My whole career depends on how I do on the tests."

So bothered am I about the emphasis on testing and its damaging effect on children that I write an article on my life as a taker of tests, which is published in *Educational Horizons* (2000). Caught up in a need to share my dismay at how school personnel are turning themselves inside out in order to meet the demands of test scores, I give a copy to Maureen.

I'm reluctant as Maureen's mentor to set myself up as a model to be copied, and yet I can't resist telling her about my experience with reading and test taking. I recall that as a beginning teacher I wasn't a paragon of the sophisticated, knowledgeable instructor of reading. Rather I was a reading enthusiast.

It was my second year of teaching, and the principal had assigned me to a below-average fifth grade (classes were organized homogeneously), which included some troublesome boys because he felt they needed a male teacher. We spent lots of time with books and became collectors searching at home for books to contribute to the class, taking biweekly trips to the public library, and soliciting the school reading specialist for book donations. We wrote to authors, dressed in the costumes of literary figures, made up plays based on book plots, and more. We played with words. I challenged the children to find a word I couldn't define, and if they were successful, I'd reward them with a pretzel. We listed our favorite poems and memorized lines we liked. The time after gym or lunch was given over to sharing a poem or story. I made a practice of reading to the class from a book I enjoyed. As they read books of their choice, I'd meet with individual children to hear their reactions to what they were reading, to note how they were handling the material, and to suggest other books they might want to read. Lo and behold, the students' scores on standardized tests soared. I didn't give it much thought. Somehow the tests took care of themselves.

My first inclination is to urge Maureen to ignore the standardized tests and to concentrate on developing a rich, vital reading program for students. I realize that kind of thinking is no longer available to Maureen. It can't be reassuring to her to hear me say, "Don't worry. Just do the best you can and the students will perform well on tests." I can't guarantee that this will be the case. Instead, Maureen and I have to face the problem of having to deal with an approach foisted on every school, every teacher, every student by a system grasping for simple solutions to complex problems.

Even though it helps to share our concerns about the inadequacies of standardized tests and to voice our support for those parents in Scarsdale, New Jersey, New York City, and elsewhere who have been protesting the idea that a single assessment can give an accurate picture of student achievement, we realize the test-taking mania is a reality. We talk about how to help children do well on exams. I suggest that she be straightforward with her students about the tests' importance but, to the extent possible, try to ease the feelings of tension. Maureen describes strategies she uses with her students that she thinks are helpful, such as writing notes on the test booklets and learning to eliminate answers that are clearly wrong.

She tells me about how she made certain her students were well nourished before taking a test by arranging for them to have breakfast together. I see that, despite her disillusionment about the undue emphasis given test scores, she searches for ways to have her classes do well. It pleases me to hear how she refused to approach test taking in a cut-and-dry manner but rather displays an understanding of the physical needs of her students. As her mentor, I let her know how gratifying it is for me to watch her take charge. Maureen is no longer the rookie responding passively to the demands of the system, but now she looks for ways to affect things for the better. She has become a valued and respected member of the faculty.

We agree that in addition to working together to create a classroom in which books and students are friends rather than adversaries, we will search out ideas from other books and people on how to help youngsters do better on standardized tests. This is in keeping with a practice we've established of sharing the results of our outside reading and of our investigation of other resources in the quest for effective approaches to educational problems. This use of the literature is an aspect of the mentorship that, I am confident, Maureen will continue practicing even after we are no longer meeting on a regular basis.

Our discussions take two different paths, one in which we see that good teaching and test preparation can overlap and another in which we find that learning to read good literature is separate from understanding how to do better on tests.

We start by coming up with ideas that don't offend our beliefs about what constitutes good teaching. They include:

- Acquainting students with different kinds of writing (e.g., nonfiction, poetry, booklets of recipes or game rules, magazine articles on various subjects, as well as fiction)
- Helping pupils distinguish between material that calls for focused reading and books that can be skimmed (e.g., guiding students to understand that seeking information in an encyclopedia takes a different kind of reading from how a story is read for pleasure)
- Encouraging students to stay at reading for longer periods by increasing the time available for in-class reading sessions
- Assisting youngsters to select books of appropriate difficulty by assuring them that it's all right to put aside a book they find uninteresting and guiding others to move to more challenging material
- Providing time for pupils to share reactions to books as a way of extending their understanding of what they've read

We also talk about techniques that may help students to score higher on the tests. For example, we can suggest to students that they read the questions first and then go back to the test passage to find the answers. We can give them experience with material that has been retyped to look as daunting and dense as test paragraphs. We can discuss with the class the differences between test questions and the way a teacher asks for responses. The teacher can spend time on helping youngsters to avoid mistakes as they move from test booklet to answer sheet.

But I remain troubled and share my concerns with Maureen. The suggestions offered in various books could provide content for an entire semester of course work for teachers with a single goal of obtaining higher test scores. I'm bothered by how much time in classrooms is being devoted to such activities as doing worksheets, deciphering the language of tests, and learning how to mark answers on a bubble sheet. I'm disturbed by the fact that standardized tests scores are used to grade teachers and schools and not to provide data lending to improved instruction and better student achievement. Teachers need to be able to study children's tests, to learn from their errors and successes.

I still believe that the reading-rich classroom will lead to better test results and—most important—to lifelong readers. As with other factors affecting teaching we have to continue dealing with what is while working with others to make changes for the better.

CHAPTER 10

The End of the Year

Maureen: A Different Kind of Energy

My students believe the year ends after they complete their standardized tests. By seventh or eighth grade they're cynical consumers of education. They know the marking period does not end in June but sometime in May. They know that all the work they do now is not accountable to the tests—those exams are now behind them. They also know, despite warnings and threats, it's going to take some kind of magic to get held over no matter what educational policy makers say about the demise of social promotion. Some failing students are mandated to attend summer school but with looming budget cuts there might be no summer program at all. For all students, though, distraction is in the air. Down coats are closeted with a pocketfull of mothballs. Tight t-shirts and provocative shorts become the order of the day. Spring fever has begun to flow through our windows, and the parade of flesh has begun.

I notice little of this, as I'm still furrowed in my first-year run. I am pacing my lessons as if I'm still in the dead of winter. When I assign Christopher Paul Curtis' *The Watsons Go to Birmingham—1963* (1999) to my seventh graders, I can't wait for my students to read the first chapter where the older brother's lips gets frozen to the car's side-view mirror in Chicago's arctic cold.

Alex raises his hand. "Is this the last book we're going to read?" he asks.

His question surprises me. Had I looked at a calendar, I would be preparing for the predictable onslaught of paperwork pertaining to class placement and report cards. Had I noticed the month, I, like Alex, would have known it was time for wrapping things up, collecting books, and adjusting the kinds of things I teach. Not the time to hand out a new book and start a new project.

Or is it?

When Sid comes, I talk about how the year has flown by and how unprepared I am for its conclusion. I tell him I need to think about ways to keep my students focused through spring fever and to extend their reading through the summer. When Alex commented about *The Watsons* being the "last book," it struck me that it might well be the last book he's going to read until he returns in the fall.

"Wouldn't it be wonderful if the kids looked to stories for comfort and didn't see reading as a chore?" I ask Sid.

He agrees. "Isn't that what we've been talking about all year? How to get kids excited about reading, how to help them see how books can add to their lives?"

While the dreamy side of me finds expression, pondering yet again about how to keep kids reading and loving it, the pragmatic me must plan curriculum that's appropriate to this time of year. It is another area I explore with Sid.

I have another startling thought as I reflect on what to do this last month in the year: What will I do without Sid?

Sid: A Different Kind of Planning

It's early June, and I join Maureen in her classroom where the teachers have begun to gather to eat their lunch. Conversation revolves around vacation plans, relief that the days of test-taking madness are over, and ways to deceive pupils into believing that classwork this last month will affect grades. One teacher suggests, "I keep them going by giving regular tests." Another says, "If things are getting out of hand, I threaten that they won't be allowed to take part in graduation exercises." As I look around, I see teachers, whose energy reserves have reached their lowest level, battling to keep students in tow despite the draw of sunny days, mild temperatures, and the sounds of life outside.

When we meet later, I tell Maureen about my own struggle to counter end-of-the-year fatigue.

> I realized that as a teacher and a principal, come June I had to find ways to recharge my batteries, to get myself going again. I searched for projects to get myself and the kids excited because they were different and interesting. With the good weather, one of the things I liked to do was to go on nature walks with my class and collect specimens to bring back to our room. I'll never forget watching praying mantises emerging from a cocoon or seeing how ants tunneled around in a dirt-filled jar or observing tadpoles changing into frogs.

But the important idea is to be aware that every teacher experiences dips and peaks of energy during the year and June brings fatigue as vacation thoughts take over.

We agree to keep thinking about ways to reenergize ourselves.

Maureen: The "Coffee House"

Sid talks about this time of year as needing a "new kind of energy." I consider his idea of nature walks, but to what end? At first, I have the students walk the neighborhood with a number 2 pencil in hand and blank paper on a clipboard or their writer's notebook. We draw what we see and write about it. We take "listening" walks and write down what we hear. I think about all those intricately drawn nature guides and consider having my students do one of those. It's hard for me to imagine that there might be an animal I might want to observe in this New York City neighborhood. Perhaps I need to show my students Barbara Bash's picture book, *Urban Roosts: Where Birds Nest in the City* (1992).

Later in the week, I notice that some teachers have fashioned educational games that review and reinforce what the students have learned all year. I admire that, but I'm not a games person. Coincidentally, end-of-the-year projects become the topic of discussions on the Teachers and Writers Collaborative Listserv (writenet@twc.org)—an e-mail discussion group about teaching literature and writing moderated by the Teachers and Writers Collaborative. I find an activity that really seems to suit me. A teacher posts an idea for a "Coffee House" where students perform creative work or share an excerpt from a favorite book. We could have snacks and a small party afterwards. We could invite parents too.

I see this plan as the perfect activity for the seventh graders while the eighth graders are away enjoying their 2-day senior trip to Boston. While the graduates are away, I will have blocks of time with the seventh graders. I also see this time as a way to invite parents into my classroom. They could bring their own favorite piece of literature or article and share too.

My principal is delighted with this plan. He could accompany the eighth graders without worrying about ongoing educational programs back home.

The kids vetoed inviting their parents.

The seventh graders throw themselves into planning, writing, and reviewing the books, magazines, and poetry they'd read during the year. I arrange time in the school library where students skim through anthologies, browse for books, sit in corners writing poetry, and find the parts of stories they want to share. We create a list of readers and elect a master of ceremonies. Two students volunteer to be photographers. One student brings a bongo drum from home to accompany himself and to beat out rhythms as he reads his poetry. Others agree to bring party goods, snacks, and soft drinks. We select decorators and organize a clean-up crew. There is a new kind of energy.

On the day of the Coffee House, seventh graders are busy creating decorations out of materials donated by the art teacher. Others are still rehearsing. Another student persuaded the computer teacher to loan him the digital camera—under supervision, of course. We borrowed a music stand from the high school and a stool from one of the science labs. Each student read or performed without a hitch, smiling and engaging and gracious. But it was when two boys—loners and struggling readers who had become friends over the year—read a poem about insects for two voices from Paul Fleischman's *Joyful Noise: Poems for Two Voices* (1988) that I melted. Their voices, which began the year childlike and high-pitched and had begun to crack and sound reedy, mellowed into melodic tenors. They enjoyed the rapt attention of their colleagues: an audience of peers to hear them out, to appreciate them, to give them approval, was something they had longed for all year, and I was happy for the opportunity for them to have it.

I wondered why it had taken me this long into the year to do something like this. The celebration had built a community of learners and readers, and it gave purpose to school work. I should do something like this often and at regular intervals. I notice the payoff of giving students the chance to work together and opportunities to develop good ideas together. In fact, I am reminded, as they are, that good ideas don't happen in isolation and that they need to get good things from each other.

I also realize there is more than one way to assess children's progress. I had developed such tunnel vision about assessment through the madness of testing days. Now I see the authenticity and value of what I observe and note about my students' development. I observe a new level of participation and engagement by my students and a new willingness to take on new verbal challenges.

I see what they have learned.

I see what I have learned.

Next year I will know better.

Maureen: Observing Sid

By June, Sid had become a member of the staff—or at least a welcome visitor. (Well before that, though, my students began to look for him on Wednesdays. When he missed one week, my students asked me where he was.) When he arrives in my area, we are lunching and watching another teacher struggle with a group of restless 12-year-olds. There's no hiding in our fishbowl. I've been observing everyone entering this room and gradually realize I'm observing Sid. I notice his patience, his self-control, the way he uses words sparingly and meaningfully. Here was a white-haired pillar of sanity. And more, he was my inspiration to never stop trying to become a better teacher.

I had black coffee with skim milk waiting for him.

He sat down. "You're taking care of me."

"How did the Coffee House go?" he asks our Resource Room teacher with whom I worked closely throughout the year.

She enthusiastically describes the project. She tells him that the sixth graders downstairs learned about the Coffee House and are looking forward to creating their own next year when they become seventh graders. She says, "It's going to become a seventh-grade tradition." My colleague praises me and lets Sid know how much fun it has been to work with me.

When my eighth graders return from their trip, they complain that there is no time for them to have a Coffee House. I wish I had done one with them earlier in the year. I learned that kids love to perform. They like having an audience, hearing applause, and celebrating.

Sid listens attentively, gently inquiring about my project so that I can hear directly the praise from my fellow teachers. I enjoy knowing that I am finally a part of the community, that I have moved from being an outsider to a valued member.

But I see too how Sid has become part of our community. All the teachers fill him in easily. No longer is he a "gentle intruder," but rather a person who inspires informed teacher talk, someone who stimulates shared thinking. I recall the days when the interns at Louis Armstrong would sit around a table and Sid would quietly bring up a topic: "And what did you think of...?" He was now doing it here, with a group of seasoned veterans and one rookie.

Sid reminds me later when we have time by ourselves that as teachers we must be—and probably are by nature—optimists. Why else do we choose to do the same thing all over again with the idea that we can do it better next year? No matter how many years we've been teaching, I've learned from talking to veteran teachers and especially with Sid, we always aspire to do better.

"It's like parenting," Sid says to me. "You always wish you could have done it differently. But when I look at my son holding his week-old daughter—and he is so good with the baby—that maybe my wife and I did something right."

And I believe he was—and is—a good parent. Not just to his own children, but to me, in guiding me, in standing by me, in reminding me through my darkest, most cynical days that this is an impossible job but one that we can do, that we can effect change and instill a love of learning, one child at a time.

Sid: Sitting Around the Table

I continue a practice of sitting with Maureen and her colleagues as they have lunch. This Wednesday when I join them, I find they are still discussing Maureen's end-of-the-year Coffee House project. I listen a while and then begin to ask questions. I always have felt comfortable doing this whether I was working with interns or meeting with teachers at the Louis Armstrong Middle School. I think the teachers appreciate the opportunity to express themselves to a neutral, external observer, someone not there to evaluate them but someone truly interested in what they have to say. I believe also that by asking questions I communicate the idea that teachers carry within them the knowledge and wisdom to provide the answers.

The teachers tell me how much the students enjoyed the Coffee House project and how others looked forward to participating next year. I ask, "Why do you think the students became so involved?" Replies come from different directions. "It was something different from what they usually do in school." "It was fun." "They were allowed to take over and it became like a party they were organizing." "They could bring in things from home as the bongo drummer did."

"Were the youngsters learning anything or just having a good time?" I inquire.

The school librarian jumps in: "All I know is that they were all over the library going through anthologies, looking through books to find the parts of stories they wanted to share, and sitting in corners writing poetry."

Maureen says, "All year long I've been worried that I haven't done a good enough job. Even though I've done a lot of work with poetry, when I saw kids struggle to write an essay about it, I thought I failed, that I hadn't given them enough words, enough hooks on which to hang their thoughts. But when I saw how they got poems ready for the Coffee House, I realized they'd learned to love poetry and that's important too."

I indicate to the teachers that from what they tell me it seems that the Coffee House gave the students an outlet for their energy and a chance for them to express their inventiveness. I think also they felt they were being treated more like adults since they were taking on roles that called for responsibility and maturity.

I ask if there are other opportunities during the year for their adolescents to channel their energy into projects like the Coffee House. An immediate response comes, "We don't have time for that kind of stuff. We've got a curriculum to cover and tests to prepare for."

I hear this comment and I'm at a loss as to what to say. I don't want to launch into a speech about young adolescents' need to engage in activities that demand responsible behavior and allow them to express who they are in different ways. I feel frustrated, but it's not the time to discuss how the drives for curriculum coverage and preparing for tests have gotten in the way of effective education. Instead, with the lunch period drawing to an end, I simply say, "There are a lot of pressures that get in the way of what you'd like to do."

Maureen has a preparation period and we go to another room to continue the conversation. I point out to her that we started talking about how the Coffee House project served to invigorate ourselves and our classes at the end of the year. But it becomes clear that it is the kind of activity that can have value throughout the year. I remind Maureen of our own shared experience at the Louis Armstrong Middle School with the community museum. There students because involved in such activities as converting the museum area into a replica of La Marqueta, the Puerto Rican market located in Manhattan, and mounting an exhibition of original haiku poetry and prints after viewing the work of Japanese children. When Maureen was an intern she helped students curate a display of life in the Rain Forest and another about Imagination and Outer Space.

We come up with other ideas about which we've heard or read. They include: setting up an exchange program with a school in another country; having an Ethnic Festival featuring the food, fashions, stories, and dances representing the backgrounds of the school's student body; starting and maintaining a school garden; organizing an arts festival; planning a dramatic presentation.

I ask Maureen to look again at what happened during the course of implementing the Coffee House project to identify any other significant events. She tells me about how two of her boys—who were shy and struggling—brought down the house with their reading of a poem for two voices. She said there was a tangible sense of the kids bringing all of themselves to school and not checking part of themselves at the door.

I share with Maureen my observation that experiences like the Coffee House give adolescents a chance to feel ownership of what's happening and to show their excitement. It gives them the opportunity to work collaboratively on a project they see as meaningful. It was fun. They were active, not passive, and they could connect their outside interests in music and photography to what was happening.

In thinking about plans for next year, we need to keep looking for activities that will elicit student interest and energy.

Maureen: Imagining a Year Without Sid

It is hard for me to think about this, but just as I must learn to wind up my curriculum with my students, I must learn to wind up my learning with Sid. What will I do without him? Our meetings have become a regular feature of my schedule, a time blocked for purposeful reflection, a deadline for logging in my notebook what I did that week and whether it went well or poorly or ways I could teach something better. I hope I'll have the discipline to maintain the practice. My log entries now focus more on my lessons, what I hope to teach next year, and I've started collecting my lessons and materials in a binder. All of this, I consider, is my work in progress.

I will miss my time debriefing with Sid, thinking out loud about a lesson or string of lessons I have done that I want to do better next year. I will miss my time talking about a new book that I have read. I will miss having a professional article placed conveniently in my hands even if I don't have a hope of having the time to read it. I will miss his attentiveness and his encouragement. I will miss his unconventional spirit that will support me in trying to do things my way, to continue to find my teaching voice. I will miss his take on the ongoing dramas of school politics both in my building and in the educational system at large.

In the meantime, we talk about some practical ways that I may continue our practice of reflection and debriefing. Here are some of our ideas:

- Take a more active role in the school's Critical Friends program. Right there I will have a cadre of supportive teachers all of whom understand that what is said in the room stays in the room. We will all practice protocols for looking at student work and we will all understand that looking at student work is for the purpose of learning to practice teaching at a more sophisticated and artful level.
- Create a teacher circle or study group. Meet with some other teachers during a common preparatory period to read something together whether it's young adult literature, a bestseller, or professional book.
- Try to buddy up with another teacher to observe and be observed. Or if I learn about someone who is doing something really well in the classroom, ask for coverage and visit that teacher. Or, try to get a partner and videotape our lessons so that we may critique ourselves.

I introduce Sid to a mentor teacher who has been assigned our school through the New Educator Support Team. The three of us arrange to meet together.

Even though I've got this list in hand, I know that I will not want to lose touch.

CHAPTER 11

What We've Learned

Maureen: Finding My Teaching Voice

When June 27 rolled around, I was the same person that walked through the doors of RFK/I.S. 250 9 months earlier, but not the same teacher. In September I stared at empty tables and imagined willing, industrious students. I peered through desks and bookshelves for clues of previous life and the schoolwork that happened here. The year was mine to make, to shape, to experience. I imagined myself, not as the stuffy, huffy Mr. K. of my own youth, but in the likeness of the loving Miss Honey in the movie version of Roald Dahl's novel, Matilda. I anticipated the sunny aspect of teaching rather than the darker realities of my new occupation.

On that day in late June, dismissing my homeroom for the last time, I'm not quite sure what to say. They were my difficult ones, the kids I'll remember to my dying day. It is my first last day. I opt for a simple goodbye and manage to squeeze in "Read!" as some bolt for the door. Others mosey on, report cards in hand, sprung from their yearly toil.

After the last student lets the door bang shut, I sit at a student desk and listen to the air settle. I can imagine the building sighing, expelling its last notes of kid sound. In the unnatural quiet of the classroom I feel old, as though I've aged more than a chronological 9 months.

My mind's eye is full of real images now: J., who came late on days I administered a test to her first-period class; R. who refused to do any work at all; P. who expressed her frustration at her misbehaving classmates. There were my girls in black sympathizing with the Columbine shooters in the discussion about the relationship between victims and bullies, and there were my specialized–high school bound. There were my poets, my engineers, my debaters, my philosophers, my rebels, and my loners. I still don't know if I'd ever step into the middle of a fight again between my students across the street from school. I recall the relationship between The Giver and Jonah in Lois Lowry's haunting tale of a memory-less society and feel the weight of memory and experience on my shoulders and in my heart.

I clean my room and find crumpled papers and wads of gum hidden between books on the lowest bookshelves, which were out of plain sight. I shake my head and mumble, "Kids!" They have left their scent behind, a warmed-up aroma of anticipation, charged with a hint of rebellion. They will go on and do what they are going to do, and I am left behind here, to clean up, to summarize, to reflect, to consider how I'll do it all again next year. It's not quite the final scene of To Sir With Love, where Sidney Poitier tears up the resignation letter he's been carrying in his front pocket after he meets a new bunch of cheeky teens but the essence is there. The sixth-grade teachers gave me a rundown about next year's group, and already I feel myself warming to the challenge. Many of the first-year teachers I know will be teaching new grades or won't be doing this again. Some others have sunk into a pool of cynicism and speak disdainfully about the children they are to teach.

Real classroom experience replaced many of my original ideas about teaching; but my career has been forever shaped by my mentor. I'll never know what kind of teacher I might have been had I not had a mentor or, specifically, had I not had Sid Trubowitz as my mentor. I do know that because I was Sid's mentee, I'll always look at teaching as an art, unique and heartfelt.

Our year began with mutual reluctance but a willingness to experiment. As Sid grappled with the directives from the Board of Education, he instituted several structures: I would keep a reflective log that he would read and respond to; we would meet regularly and those meetings would address my needs; I would be free to set the agenda and Sid would respond; I could call Sid any time or e-mail him; Sid would make himself a familiar face in my classroom—he would participate with group work but would not model lessons.

Our relationship grew over time. Sid's nonjudgmental and supportive attitude encouraged me to let go of my steel layer of first-year protection. Even though I had known Sid previously through my work as an intern, I had not worked with him so intimately. I found that as we continued to work together, trust between us developed. During those first observations I felt like a performer—and perhaps all the way through the lessons that failed. His response of encouragement and support reassured me that I did not have to prove my worth to him and that it was important to keep my head about things, to remember above all my own common sense.

Over time I was able to transform from performer (or failed performer) to my real self, warts and all, in front of kids. My views of Sid's weekly observation also transformed; they moved from being a nerve-wracking addition to my overloaded schedule to a comforting, predictable structure where I knew I could get reliable and honest feedback about my pedagogy. And it was only then, after experiencing all the steps of the transition, that I could arrive at a place where I could begin to assemble the elements of my own teaching voice.

A turning point for me as a mentee was a lesson when students took the conversation in a direction that was important to them and I redirected when necessary. Sid wrapped up the lesson for me and demonstrated the importance of praising kids for their involvement, their courage, and their willingness to share. Later, he highlighted the moment for me; it was a time when kids brought their full selves to a discussion. It was not a time when, as I have felt so often, they checked their minds at the door, in much the same way that Doug Buehl describes in his book *Classroom Strategies for Interactive Learning* (2001). Students, he argues, divide their minds into "world brains" and "school brains." The world brain, he explains, "is where the student keeps all of what he knows and understands about the world." In contrast, the school brain "has a minuscule storage capacity....The most distinctive feature of the school brain is an ever-open chute, ready to dump yesterday's lesson quickly and irrevocably into oblivion" (p. 17). During that period students integrated their world brains and school brains for a vivid learning experience.

Morever, that just as teachers should plan curriculum that brings together the world brain and the school brain of the students, mentors and mentees need to adhere to similar principles. Important learning experiences for new teachers involve those times that they too bring their whole brains into the classrooms, not just their school brains.

The regularity of Sid's visits and conversation around teaching enabled me to move faster away from the many habits of the novice. For example, I took everything personally. When Sid advised me to practice the important skill of having children speak to one another instead of just to the teacher, I initially took it as a personal criticism. It took time—and a lot of conversation around that issue—for me to realize it was not personal but professional. Sid helped me visualize a teaching persona—that a professional voice might borrow parts of my true self, but might also represent a collection of teaching methods that I felt philosophically at one with.

Similarly, it took time—and again plenty of discussion —about taking adolescent student behavior (and the cutting comments they make) less personally. While I learned (again through talking it out with Sid) that it's okay to be angry with kids, it is just as important for me not to get snagged by their mind games or be easily provoked by their hormonal ups and downs. In other words, I learned to "read" kids better, to see beyond their behavior, to understand better what I was observing.

As the year progressed, my thinking moved beyond issues of basic needs to deeper issues of pedagogy. Our relationship transformed too. We moved from near strangers uncomfortable with our assigned roles to colearners. For example, when testing issues came to the table, we looked back in our personal histories to what we both knew from experience as students and, in Sid's case, from his years of teaching experience. But we both knew that educators are engaged in dialogue about testing and so together we read and discussed other professional books and articles.

Through reading, Sid and I enhanced our expertise on matters ranging from the types of standardized tests to concrete ways we could help kids prepare for them better. Even though Sid did not himself have to cope with the issues of standardized testing in his own classroom and, in fact, felt the impulse to stand up and speak out against this trend, he participated with me as if in a study group. It taught me that through knowledge, investigation, and inquiry—and a teaching buddy—I could strike a satisfying balance between what was required of me by the system and what I needed for my own personal expression as an instructor. He had given me the secret of longevity in my career, the secret of how not to be beaten down by a system that often operates by brute force.

We also began to understand more about how teachers develop in response to external pressure, and we mapped out teacher development in stages. In our initial response to professional demands, we teachers almost always think back to what we know, to what we experienced as students, and do the same in our classrooms. If there is no external support—staff developer, mentor, professional study group, or appropriate school culture—teachers are unlikely to expand their practice. Teachers who are pressured to perform without professional development do what they know just to get it done. It takes time and talk for teachers to develop, and it cannot be done by an individual alone.

Because I was in a mentor-mentee relationship, developing my practice was top priority. I would allocate time to consider alternative approaches, involve myself in professional discussions with other teachers, and investigate the larger thinking about a topic through professional literature. My professional development time was sacrosanct. This became a habit and shaped not just my first year, but all my subsequent years as well.

Mentoring shaped my career in several other ways as well:

• So much of becoming a teacher for me that first year involved integrating my idealism with the practical realities of the profession. I had dreamt about all those willing learners only to discover rebellious teens rejecting knowledge at every pass. I had dreamt about a beautiful classroom with new books on shelves and lots of reading going on;

my reality involved limited supplies, cramped quarters, and kids who hated to read. What I learned from my mentor was not to let the dreams die, but to unpack ways to slip them into my reality. Similarly, I could immerse myself in educational theory, but I had to find a way to unpack it for kids and put into practice.

- Like all new teachers I've had my share of ups and downs, victories and failures. Unmentored teachers often suffer these extremes— defeats and successes—but experience them alone behind the closed classroom door. I enjoyed the perspective of an outsider sharing with me new ways to consider a particular event. I might have had a difficult lesson, but Sid named the small successes that he saw and I did not. There were days when this made a lot of difference for me.

- Having a mentor has kept me out of trouble and prevented me from falling in with the "wrong crowd." I avoided teachers who viewed the kids as lost causes, as well as those who simply did the minimum. Many young teachers are taken under the wing of veteran instructors who pass down a culture of indifference. That might be true with some mentors, too, but not in my case.

- It's easy to begin a teaching career full of idealism and enthusiasm and by year's end sink into a mire of cynicism and self-doubt. I've often written in my log to Sid that I worry that I haven't done a good enough job. In one instance he responded: "The agony of teaching is that we always feel that there is something more we could have done. A score on a test can't measure what we do for kids. I know you've given your classes a lot when I see them with their noses buried in books and eagerly exchanging ideas." And on another occasion he wrote, "Our impact on them shows years later." Thus Sid offered me the gift of perspective: I've got to consider what I do as the accumulation of my days, not just one day or one year separate and apart from the next.

In all of these ways, beyond examining my first year, Sid doled out a method for viewing my teaching as a workable, changeable thing, so that year after year of a career in teaching is not a death sentence but the challenge of keeping myself excited as a learner and making compromises with the system. It is that negotiation between the demands of the system and what keeps me excited as a learner that will shape my teaching voice.

I shut out the lights and carry books and keys for the last time as a first-year teacher. Teachers gravitate to the office and linger, making last-minute phone calls, turning in keys, signing off, exchanging phone numbers. I'll be better next year, but I feel stronger knowing I've got Sid's e-mail address on the desktop of my home computer.

Sid: The Mentorship Ends

The year has ended. But it's not really over. I'll continue to see and speak to Maureen. We've been writing together, recapitulating our experience and for now that keeps us in touch. I know that we will always be professional colleagues who will find time to talk about what we're doing in schools.

I started working with Maureen not knowing what to expect, with concerns that I'd be swamped with demands for reports and expected to operate in a prescribed manner. I worried that whatever I did would prove futile in the face of too large classes, inadequate classroom space, and the specter of tests lurking in the background. I wondered if all I could realistically accomplish would be to keep Maureen's head above water for the year and for her not to flee to a suburban school or to another profession.

I came to the mentorship with a measure of confidence. After all, I'd been a teacher, assistant principal, principal, professor, and educator for over 40 years. But underneath it all I felt a bit of trepidation. I suspected that public school staff might look at me as one of those college professors with his head in the clouds. They would lump me with the education faculty of their college courses, who taught them nothing about roll books, lesson plans, ways to control students, and how to get better test scores. Their unspoken words might be: "You haven't been a public school teacher for years and your experience as a principal was at a different time in a different area. What do you know about helping a teacher in a Queens middle school?"

This view of me as a nonpractical character from a university campus had been reinforced when I applied to the Board of Education to be a mentor for new principals and was turned down. My years mentoring administrators, teachers, and interns at the Louis Armstrong Middle School carried no weight with those who made the decision. Even though I had been a principal of a Harlem elementary school and had taught courses in educational administration for many years, they considered me too removed from the real world of schools to be effective as a mentor. I didn't know the forms that needed to be filled out, how to prepare teachers and students for tests, ways to set up schedules. I came as an anomaly, a professor of education speaking a different language. I hadn't been a part of their bureaucratic world.

Beginning to work with Maureen presented fewer obstacles. I knew her from the Louis Armstrong Middle School where she had been an intern. We both were part of a school where a different ethos existed, where teachers and professors operated as colleagues, where mutual respect replaced condescension and suspicion. I had a head start with Maureen but it was still going to be a challenge—meeting every week, different kids, intense talk, and a school where nobody knew me.

I plunged ahead and began a year of viewing Maureen's classes from a cramped corner of a crowded room, joining with her and the students as they discussed matters ranging from bullying to ways to tell others about the books they've read, thinking with Maureen about what was happening during my time in her class, and sharing ideas with her about schools, students, and the educational system.

Our first meetings were a place for Maureen to pour out her feelings: anger at parents who didn't know what their children were doing after school; annoyance at students who cheated, were vicious to each other, didn't do their homework; irritation at teachers who tried to shift their responsibility to her shoulders; uncertainty about how to deal with other people in the school; worries about how to handle her emotional reactions to youngsters.

These beginning sessions called upon me to show restraint. How easy it would have been to deliver messages from on high, to fall into the role of guru. It would have been a simple matter to stand on a mountaintop and point the way to teaching perfection. But I didn't have to work with students on a day-to-day basis, getting them ready for tests. I didn't have to face what can be adolescent irrationality, the sometimes inappropriate expression of hormonal eruption. I didn't have to encounter parents who used the school as a target for their frustrations.

I kept trying to put myself in Maureen's shoes and thought back to my own experiences so that I could come close to feeling what she felt. I didn't want to talk about my successes as a teacher without also identifying the frustrations I experienced. My own internal mentor reminded me that it was Maureen's concerns, questions, and problems that would provide the framework for our meetings, emphasizing the importance of listening, cautioning me to be wary of saying things only to show how smart I was, to enhance my status, or to prove my value.

Every Wednesday we met and our relationship grew bit by bit. There was no magical moment when we realized that we had become a team and had grown to trust each other. There was no single event that made up the emotional and intellectual scaffolding supporting our mentorship. Rather it was the hours of participating directly in Maureen's classroom, joining in activity, listening, and observing. It was being present to hear an angry parent complain about the treatment her child was receiving. It was feeling the excitement of youngsters given leeway to express themselves, describing how they fit in with the school and with others. It was noting how a veteran teacher subverted Maureen's authority by reprimanding one of her students in front of her. It was being part of all these happenings and more. Seeing with my own eyes and hearing with my own ears gave me the unfiltered, detailed impressions that told me how things were going for Maureen.

In our discussions we kept coming back to the whys of doing what we do, to being clear about purpose, and to searching for the causes of behavior. Why do we have students read out loud? What are the purposes of parent-teacher conferences? What are the causes of fighting, cheating, or other forms of deviant behavior? I knew that we had become thinking partners who probe beneath the surface of what teachers do in the classroom when after one of our sessions Maureen sent me the following e-mail: "At times I wish I had the exact formula to apply, but I know we've taken the right direction, constantly thinking and rethinking about ways to reach the most challenging kids, the most at-risk students, the ones who have never liked reading because they did it slower or it took them longer."

It wasn't long before I could tell upon entering Maureen's room if things had been going badly. On these occasions, when I asked how things were going, Maureen would release a stream of concern—students who haven't done their homework; boys ridiculing gays by making their voices sound effeminate; and to top it off, word from the main office that she had to be reinterviewed to retain her job for next year. At times like this I saw myself as someone who lifts the top off a boiling kettle, allowing the steam to escape.

I learned that one of the ways I could be of most use to Maureen was to help her deal with the emotions that accompany teaching. I assured her it was all right to feel resentment towards J., with her constant accusations of unfairness, to become mad at T. for his bullying of smaller boys, or to feel upset about Mrs. K. who seemed not to care about her daughter. I pointed out to her that there may be children in her classes she may not like and others she may not be able to reach. I let her know that she is allowed to have feelings of anger or disappointment and they don't represent flaws in her as a teacher or as a person.

As the year progressed, our meetings took on a different tone. Maureen no longer had a pressing need to deal only with the problem of the day. We talked also about merit pay, learning styles, ways to evaluate students that go beyond numerical grading, and how to involve parents in their children's education—issues teachers and schools everywhere are facing. At other times we told each other about the books we'd been reading, the movies we'd seen, and the concerts we'd attended. We interacted as two people dedicated to their professions and interested in the world around them.

When we had these exchanges, and if I'd see a buildup of pressure in her tired eyes and sagging shoulders, I would urge Maureen, if she could, to try to find balance in her life as she weighed the demands of being teacher, parent, and wife. I knew this was not easy. I shared my own memories as a beginner coming home to collapse with fatigue after a day of physical and emotional draining. I described how I sought ways to relax and to find sustenance in such activities as bike riding, leisure reading, long walks, and movies. I hoped our talks would help her to keep searching for that place between total school involvement and an outside life.

Other changes occurred. At first I was the superior communicating out of years of experience and accumulated knowledge. I was the one reminding Maureen not to repeat student answers, pointing out ways to get youngsters to interact with each other rather than always directing responses to the teacher, and stressing the need for careful preparation before breaking the class into groups.

But as teachers and schools faced new major problems like how to deal with the pressure for good test scores, a problem that was absent from my own experience, we became collaborators in the search for answers. We read different books and shared what we found. We read the same book and discussed what we saw. We looked at what other schools were doing and collected ideas that we could incorporate without violating our educational beliefs. We gave in to reality and came up with a series of test-taking tips that we could give students to help them score better.

As we worked together, I watched in awe as Maureen demonstrated her skill in using the computer. She was able to network with colleagues throughout the country, to find resources to expand her teaching repertoire, and to involve students in gathering research material. I came from a different generation and didn't grow up with computers, so I was glad for the opportunity to draw on her expertise, as were the school administrators who have called upon her on a number of occasions to train other teachers.

In the middle of the year I felt hungry for contact with other mentors and visited a Bronx school where a number of them were operating. They told me about the new teachers with whom they were working whose strengths were not nearly like those possessed by Maureen. They described them this way: "He's totally unambitious. Never goes to the library for materials." "She flies by the seat of her pants. Planning is not part of her vocabulary." "The woman I'm paired with has limited basic knowledge. Her grammar is poor and her spelling is weak."

My trip to the Bronx reinforced for me the recognition that in Maureen I had an unusual mentee. She is a mother, has worked at other jobs, and is creative and intelligent. I realized that in working with other mentees I might have to operate in a different manner. For many the goal would be survival. I would need to provide specific suggestions, to focus on minimal norms of expected behavior, and to deal with how to handle the first day and the first week. But even in these cases I would stress understanding, not tricks. I know that if I were to begin working with another new teacher, my first task would be to "read" the mentee and proceed from there.

I considered what I would do with the mentees described by the Bronx mentors. In the case of the newcomer with language deficits I'd have her write, write, write, and together we'd find ways to improve. For the mentee described as "unambitious" and the one who ignores planning, I'd probe beneath the behavior to find the reasons for the lack of involvement. Always I'd look for ways to generate excitement and to help them get satisfaction from what they do.

When I read about the numbers of new teachers starting in schools and the requirement for all to have mentors, I wonder if there are enough people of maturity, experience, insight, and interest ready to take on the task of helping someone grow as a professional. It's easy to list the characteristics of good mentoring—professional, positive, collegial, responsive, supportive, empathic, and nonevaluative—but unless they are applied in a sensitive, imaginative manner, they become devoid of meaning. I think also about possible obstacles to effective mentoring. I have heard about veteran teachers who, against their will, are pressured by administrators into working with novices. There are others for whom gaining a power position is the primary motivation and still others who view mentoring as the job of cloning themselves. Then there are the problems identified by mentors who find themselves affected by how others perceive their role in professional development. Some bristle at the notion of having to fix problem teachers or to implement new directives or mandates from district offices. I point to potential problems, not to negate mentoring—for this kind of support is necessary and can be invaluable—but only to suggest that it be planned and implemented with care.

It was June and at Wendy's over coffee, as we had done on so many Wednesdays, we reviewed the day's experience. This time, however, we also took the time to plan for next year. As always the informality of the place and the absence of interruption made for an easy flow of ideas. Maureen and I together had succeeded in bringing thinking into a culture primarily devoted to doing. In looking at the year ahead, I reminded Maureen that although I would not be her mentor, she had already begun to develop her own mentoring community. She had joined a Critical Friends group where colleagues served as sounding boards for each other. She had found like-minded people with whom she had lunch, who enjoyed exploring school matters. I pointed out that the value of sitting around and discussing views with others ought not to be underestimated. I recalled my own experience with a college group that met weekly over a period of years to plan, implement, and assess the Queens College collaboration with the New York City Board of Education at the Louis Armstrong Middle School. For me these were my golden years in education so satisfying were the results and the chance to share.

With our year drawing to a close, I think about how far Maureen has come. Her worry about her job at I.S. 250 proved needless. She was reinterviewed and rehired. She is now looked at as an important member of the faculty. She is seen as someone who carries out interesting projects, and has the respect of other teachers, parents, and students. Others have recognized her ability. For example, she has been invited to take part in a program sponsored by the Academy of American Poets to create curriculum inte-grating poetry and technology. She is being recruited by other school sys-tems. At Queens College she has been asked to work with a group of fel-lows, the new teachers hired by the New York City Board of Education. But more than this evidence of how she has grown in stature in her school and more than the outside acknowledgment of her achievements is what has happened to her as a teacher.

As I sat with her earlier in an empty classroom and teachers came in to return a book or just say hello, I was reminded of all the connections Maureen had made over the year. She has created a colleague community here at the school, with the teachers participating in the Academy of American Poets project, and with me, her mentor. She has overcome the limitations of the locked-door classroom to meet with others to discuss what teaching is all about. Thinking about schools and students has become part of her day. She's expanded her view of the teacher's world. A book by Lucy Calkins, a pronouncement coming out of Washington mandating tutoring for students in failing school, a budget cut and the subsequent loss of art programs, the annual publication of test scores all affect what happens to her and her students. They matter to her and she talks with others about what to do.

It's not easy for new ideas to be absorbed and become part of who you are. But I know that the thoughts Maureen and I have shared about middle school youngsters, curriculum, and her reactions to events have now become part of how she thinks and acts. She knows that she can have a range of feelings about how things are going and by not being hard on her-self find ways to make them better. She no longer worries that she is a poor teacher when things go wrong. An activity that doesn't connect with stu-dents becomes grist for learning, not proof that she is inadequate. She asks questions like these: "Why didn't things go the way they were planned?" and "What could I do differently the next time?" Risk taking is okay, and if things don't go well, no tragedy.

I watched Maureen's view of curriculum expand. When bongo playing and photography became part of the Coffee House project, her classes came alive. Energy filled the room as students talked about issues that mattered to them, about bullying, feeling like an outsider, how people treat each other. Maureen saw the atmosphere change when youngsters were able to blur the differences between school studies and real-world experiences. As they brought their outside lives into the room, she began to see them as more complete people and to understand better what they needed.

Maureen didn't come to teaching as a blank tablet. She brought many assets with her. But our year of sharing ideas, trying different things, mak-ing mistakes, and finding successes have come together to create someone who believes in herself as a teacher. She has a clearer set of ideas, her sense of self is stronger, she has become a true professional.

As for me, I haven't had to keep in touch with what is happening in education only through newspaper reports and magazine articles. Each Wednesday as I passed the security guard booth, walked through hallways filled with adolescent vigor, and met with Maureen and sometimes with her colleagues, I recaptured a feeling of optimism that we can make a difference through our schools. When I think about my year with Maureen, I am renewed in my belief that despite not having been a public school teacher or administrator for a long time I can be relevant, that I am still able to understand the current problems of teachers and schools, that I can identify with a newcomer's struggle to define herself as a teacher.

I am grateful to Maureen for she has given me a gift, a gift that teachers everywhere crave, the feeling that what I've done has had a payoff. When I read Maureen's recapitulation of our time together, I look with admiration at someone who allowed herself to be vulnerable, who opened herself to an outsider. I think back fondly to our table here at Wendy's where we pondered how to get parents involved in their children's education, how to get youngsters excited about books, how to find sources to nourish our minds and spirits, and how to deal with the problems of education, large and small.

I recall my own mentors—Bertha Padouk, the reading teacher at P.S. 154 in Queens, who helped a 25-year-old novice to believe in himself as a teacher and his ability to contribute to others; John Ames, former dean of the Queens College School of Education, avuncular and kind, who presented a model of optimism and support that was invaluable for a beginning professor; Saul Cohen, the former president of Queens College, whose leadership provided me with the opportunity to mesh my experience in public schools with what I was doing at the university and for 20 years to be involved in the Queens College–Louis Armstrong Middle School Collaboration; and Seymour Sarason, who models for me the mentor who sees his role as a helper but also as learner, whose insights about education continue to astonish me, and to whom, to this day, I can turn to for counsel and be confident in his wise judgment.

I tell Maureen our lines of communication—e-mail, telephone, personal meetings—will never be closed and each of us, when there is a need, can contact the other. As our formal relationship concludes, I think of Virgil's words to Dante (*Purgatorio*, Canto XXVII, lines 140–142, p. 271) as the Pilgrim's journey draws to an end:

> *Your own will is whole, upright, and free*
> *and it would be wrong not to do as it bids you,*
> *therefore I crown and mitre you over yourself.*

Sid's Checklist for Mentors

- Mentors recognize that mentoring is a process of enabling another to act, and of building on the mentee's strengths rather than imposing ideas and information from the outside.
- Mentors not only focus on teaching techniques but also on the development of the mentee as an individual in interaction with students.
- The mentoring relationship allows frustration, anger, and other emotions to be expressed.
- Mentors are storytellers who relate back to their own beginning teaching to gain a deeper understanding of what the mentee is experiencing.
- Mentors make provision for thinking to be shared between meetings through the use of e-mail and the telephone.
- Mentors are aware of their own feelings so that any inclination to maintain status does not take precedence over the needs of the mentee.
- Mentors participate in classroom activity as a way of understanding better what the mentee is doing and feeling.
- Mentors talk about the books they've read, the plays and movies they've seen, and their other interests and encourage the mentee to do the same.
- Mentors establish an atmosphere in which the mentee feels free to take risks.
- Mentors raise questions that go beyond issues of day-to-day survival.
- Mentors encourage the mentee to find professional stimulation from others, such as Critical Friends groups, colleagues, and educational organizations.
- Mentors are open to learning from mentees who may have strengths they do not have. At times, the mentorship is a process of mutual appropriation rather than a simple transmission of knowledge.

- Mentors encourage the mentee to look inward by keeping a log and also maintain logs for themselves.
- Mentors recognize that mentees are at different levels of development and adjust their approach accordingly.
- Mentors avoid overidealizing their own past experience and are aware of the changing reality of the present.
- Mentors express their values regarding such current trends in education as standards-based curriculum, the implementation of business practices, and the use of vouchers.
- Mentors serve as cheerleaders, modeling enthusiasm and optimism and providing support at times of discouragement.
- Mentors help others such as school administration to recognize the mentee's worth.
- Mentors believe in the importance of listening and giving total attention as the mentee works toward becoming a skilled professional.

Maureen's List of Do's and Don'ts for Mentors

- *Do* listen to mentees and transform their ideas into workable lessons.
- *Don't* give mentees lesson plans and sheets that are not related to what they seem to be trying to do. Apprise yourself of schoolwide instructional initiatives and adhere to those goals.
- *Don't* pressure mentees to reteach lesson plans you created.
- *Do* give tips to mentees on how to create authentic and workable lesson plans.
- *Don't* assume mentees are not interested in having you in the classroom. Sometimes mentees need the time from September to December to figure out what they need to know.
- *Don't* jump in during observations and commandeer the class. Have the patience and courtesy to wait until the end of the lesson and a time when you and your mentee can confer privately.
- *Do* become a novice at something to develop empathy for your mentee and remember what it's like to be a brand new teacher.
- *Do* keep a log. Your example helps mentees maintain a progress portfolio of their own growth as teachers.
- *Do* model good listening. Sit back and encourage the mentee's contribution.
- *Do* read books and talk about them with your mentee. Conversation will gravitate toward higher levels of ideas and literacy.
- *Do* stay positive. By talking up things that the mentee is doing correctly, you will reinforce good teaching practice and build the novice's self-esteem.

Maureen's List of Do's and Don'ts for Mentees

- *Don't* take offense if your mentor jumps in. Mentors don't mean to be offensive, just proactive. They may be over enthusiastic or miss being in their own classrooms.
- *Do* keep an eye out for another person on the staff who might be a natural mentor for you.
- *Don't* get frustrated if your specialty is language arts and you are matched with the retired science teacher. While mentors from other subject areas may have little to offer in the way of content area expertise, they might have some keen ideas about skill building or classroom management.
- *Do* figure out what your mentor has to offer and take all of it.
- *Do* "kid watch" when your mentor models a lesson. Monitoring kid reaction will help you refine the approach you see in a way you feel is more useful.
- *Do* use video and audio tape-recording equipment in order to revisit classroom activities and to learn from what you see and hear.
- *Do* keep a log. Your thoughts and what you discussed with your mentor provide much material for you to consider.
- *Do* listen. Make eye contact, sit knee to knee, and be ready to respond to what your mentor is saying.

References

General References

Dante Alighieri. (2001). *The inferno, a new verse translation by W.S. Merwin.* New York: Alfred A. Knopf.

Atwell, N. (1987). *In the middle: Writing, reading, and learning with adolescents.* Portsmouth, NH: Heinemann.

Board of Education of the City of New York. (1997). New standards performance standards for English language arts. New York, NY.

Buehl, D. (2001). *Classroom strategies for interactive learning.* Newark, DE: International Reading Association.

Calkins, L., Montgomery, K., & Santmann, D., with Falk, B. (1998). *A teacher's guide to standardized reading tests.* Portsmouth, NH: Heinemann.

Daniels, H. (1994). *Literature circles: Voice and choice in the student-centered classroom.* York, ME: Stenhouse.

Darling-Hammond, L. (2000). *Solving the demands of teacher supply, demands, and starndards: What can states and school districts do?* Washington, DC: National Commission on Teaching and America's Future.

Gardner, H. (1999). *The disciplined mind: What all students should understand.* New York: Simon & Shuster.

Goodnough, A. (2002, February 13). The struggle to find enough teaching mentors. *The New York Times,* Section 8, 9.

John Steiner, V. (2000). *Creative collaboration.* New York: Oxford University Press.

Kazin, A. (1979). *A walker in the city.* New York: Harcourt, Brace.

McCourt, F. (2002, April 14). Education life supplement, *The New York Times.*

Trubowitz, S. (1984). *When a college works with a public school.* Boston: The Institute for Responsive Education.

Trubowitz, S. (2000). My life with tests. *Educational Horizons,* 79(1).

Young Adult Literature

Anderson, L. H. (1999). *Speak.* New York: Farrar, Straus & Giroux.

Bemelmans, L. (1939). *Madeline.* New York, New York: Simon & Schuster.

Bash, B. (1992). *Urban roosts: Where birds nest in the city.* Boston: Little, Brown.

Crutcher, C. (1995). *Ironman*. New York: Random House.

Curtis, C. P. (1997). *The Watsons go to Birmingham–1963*. New York: Bantam Doubleday Dell.

Fleischman, P. (1988). *Joyful noise: Poems for two voices*. New York: Harper Collins.

Freedman, R. (1993). *Eleanor Roosevelt: A life of discovery*. New York: Clarion.

Glenn, M. (1996). *Who killed Mr. Chippendale? A mystery in poems*. New York: Lodestar.

Hawthorne, N. (1967). *The house of seven gables*. New York: Bantam Classic. (Originally published in 1851)

Hinton, S. E. (1967). *The outsiders*. New York: Viking Penguin.

Lowry, L. (1993). *The giver*. New York: Bantam Doubleday Dell.

Murphy, J. (1993). *Across America on an emigrant train*. New York: Clarion.

Warren, Andrea (1997). *Orphan train rider: One boy's true story*. New York: Scholastic.

Suggested Readings

Ayers, W. (2001). *To teach—The Journey of a Teacher* (2nd ed.). New York: Teachers College Press.

In this book William Ayers presents his view of teaching by connecting personal experience with the task of guiding children into a better understanding of themselves and the world in which they live. His writing is thoughtful, imaginative, and eloquent. He gives the prospective teacher a vision of what schools and teaching could be and provides much food for thought for the new teacher seeking to develop an individual teaching voice.

Ayers, W. (Ed.). (1995). *To become a teacher.* New York: Teachers College Press.

This collection of well-written articles by Maxine Greene, Joseph Featherstone, William Ayers, and others provides a vision of what the new teacher may encounter as he or she begins a professional career. The writers also paint a picture of what schools could be like if imagination, dedication, and intelligence are applied to the effort to teach children.

Black, S. (2001). A lifeboat for new teachers. *American School Board Journal, 188*(9), 46–48.

This article emphasizes the need for a carefully planned program of mentoring. It points to a 1966 analysis by the National Commission on Teaching and America's Future (Teachers College, Columbia University) that indicates a poor mentoring program contributes to lower levels of effectiveness for teachers who remain in their jobs and higher rates of new-teacher attrition. Quoting John Goodlad, who says, "New teachers are being closeted out there with mentors—the very people some of us think ought to be doing a better job," Susan Black supports his recommendation that it would be a good idea to mentor the mentors before matching them with new teachers.

Boreen, J., Johnson, M. K., Niday, D., & Potts, J. (2000). *Mentoring beginning teachers: Guiding, reflecting, coaching.* York, ME: Stenhouse.

The authors provide suggestions on how to work with new teachers, interspersed with observations of the novice professionals. The book mixes ideas on working with student teachers with views on how to interact with beginning classroom instructors.

Brock, B.L., & Grady, M.L. (2001). *From first-year to first-rate: Principals guiding beginning teachers* (2nd ed.). Thousand Oaks, CA: Corwin Press.
    Directed at principals, this book suggests ways to help new teachers. Research is referred to frequently and, at times, in a very dry fashion. Some suggestions are too general to be of much help.

Codell, E.R.(1999). *Educating Esme: Diary of a teacher's first year.* Chapel Hill, NC: Algonquin Books.
    Esme Raji Codell describes her first year as a new teacher in an engaging manner. Her encounters with administrators, other teachers, parents, and the youngsters provide much material for discussion. Of particular interest is the fact that she connects her class's high test scores with the many interesting things she did with them during the year.

Crow, G.M., & Matthews, L. J. (1998). *Finding one's way: How mentoring can lead to dynamic leadership.* Thousand Oaks, CA: Corwin Press.
    This book combines a scholarly approach including frequent references to research with common sense ideas. The plethora of information provided at times makes it difficult to absorb. These ideas are to be studied rather than internalized.

Fletcher, R. (1993). *What a writer needs.* Portsmouth, NH: Heinemann.
    This instructive book on how to teach writing offers a writer's view on mentors. Each description of a writer's need shows what a teaching mentor should be, for example, "A Mentor Builds on Strength."

Gawandi, A. (2002, January, 28). The learning curve. *The New Yorker,* pp. 52–61.
    This is a fascinating article describing the path a new surgeon takes as he learns to become proficient in his profession. "Like everyone else, surgeons need practice. That's where you come in" can also be applied to teaching. Although Gawandi tells about the slips and stumbles of the newcomer to surgery, his words remind us that the new teacher also experiences problems and makes mistakes as he or she learns to teach.

John-Steiner, V. (1985). *Notebooks of the mind: Explorations of thinking* (pp.13–37). Albuquerque, NM: University of New Mexico Press.
    The chapter on apprenticeships contains ideas that can be related to the development of a mentorship. John-Steiner provides examples of how creative expression is nurtured and evolves. She points to numerous examples of the value of a model in stimulating the curiosity and interests of a younger person.

John-Steiner, V. (2000). *Creative collaboration.* New York: Oxford University Press.
    This book does a fascinating job of describing the value and variations of collaborating. John-Steiner devotes an entire chapter to mentoring, using illus-

trations from various fields. The book is filled with rich ideas and concepts as it discusses vertical collaborations, thought communities, and collaborations across generations. The material has been garnered through numerous interviews and the study of the lives of creative individuals.

National Education Association. (1996, July). *Building parent partnerships* (NEA Teacher-to-Teacher Book). Washington, DC: Author.
This booklet tells the stories of how teachers have attempted to facilitate parent-teacher communication. They discuss what worked and what didn't work. They provide diagrams, checklists, and tables that teachers may find useful.

Parini, J. (2002, February 25). Saluting all the king's mentors. *The New York Times*, p. E1.
In this article Parini describes how important mentors have been to his development as a writer. His insights can also be applied to teaching. He offers a number of rich ideas. For example, he writes this about his mentor: "He was generous, too, and understood that praise and censure have to be carefully meted out so that the younger writer doesn't lose hope. It is just so miserably easy to lose hope."

Portner, H. (1998). *Mentoring new teachers.* Thousand Oaks, CA: Corwin Press.
Hal Portner breaks down mentoring into four functions: Relating, Assessing, Coaching, and Guiding. He provides various exercises to illustrate ways of implementing these functions. What he presents can be useful in stimulating thought and discussion regarding what constitutes effective mentoring. If the mentor probes more deeply into himself or herself, then the book has proved valuable.

Portner, H. (2001). *Training mentors is not enough: Everything else schools and districts need to do.* Thousand Oaks, CA: Corwin Press.
As the title implies, this is a more general look at mentorships. Not only does it examine the role of the mentor and mentee, but it also discusses such topics as the involvement of higher education, evaluation of mentorship programs, school district responsibility in the development of mentorship programs, and how other activities can support the goals of mentorships. The book can serve as a reminder to schools of items to consider in planning mentorships.

Rowley, J. B. (1999). Supporting new teachers. *Educational Leadership, 56*(8), 20–22.
In this article James B. Rowley identifies six basic qualities of the good mentor: (1) The mentor is committed to the role of mentoring and has the benefit of formal training; (2) the mentor is accepting of the new teacher and approaches him or her in a nonjudgmental way; (3) the mentor is skilled at providing instructional support; (4) the mentor is skillful at interpersonal relations; (5) the men-

tor models continuous learning by attending conferences and by ongoing professional reading; and (6) the mentor communicates hope and optimism. Throughout the article Rowley suggests references to assist in the development of the qualities he identifies.

Scherer M. (Ed.). (1999). A better beginning: Supporting and mentoring new teachers. Alexandria, VA: Association for Supervision and Curriculum Development.
    This book is organized around different sections: What Do New Teachers Need; Creating an Induction Program; Making Mentoring Meaningful; Planning Comprehensive Teacher Support; Improving Instruction and Communication; Listening to Teachers. The chapters provide a comprehensive picture of mentoring programs being instituted across the country as well as addressing how to expand a new teacher's repertoire of effective teaching strategies.

Scott, J. (2002, April 21). Once bitten, twice shy: A world of eroding trust. *The New York Times*, p. D5.
    Although this article relates the idea of trust to a number of large issues, it contains some nuggets that are applicable to the mentor-mentee relationship: "Trust tends to be built slowly, through small steps. It is fragile. In everything from diplomacy to intimacy, it is easier to obliterate than to create"; and "It demands vulnerability and grows through small risks. And it grows when those risks are reciprocated....A friend reveals something personal, it is matched, trust deepens."

Shea, G. F. (1997). *Mentoring: How to develop successful mentor behaviors* (rev. ed.). Menlo Park, CA: Crisp Publications.
    In this book Gordon F. Shea gives ideas on how to develop effective mentor behaviors, dealing with what makes mentoring special and assesses what the mentor is able and willing to invest in the relationship. This thoughtful book presents insights into the mentor role and assists the prospective mentor to visualize the task by relating back to experience.

Tharp, R. G., & Gallimore, R. (1988). *Rousing minds to life: Teaching, learning, and schooling in social context*. New York: Cambridge University Press.
    The authors explore the task of providing continuous training and skillful assistance to promote teacher growth. They describe in detail procedures for enhancing teacher performance including didactic instruction, modeling and role-playing, feedback via videotape, direct coaching via an earphone, and other forms of feedback.

Trubowitz, S. (2000). My life with tests. *Educational Horizons, 79*(1), 38–40.
    In this article, Sid Trubowitz describes his lifetime of experience with taking

tests. He takes us from his elementary school days through junior high school and high school to his beginnings as a professional educator.

Trubowitz, S. (1972). The tyranny of time. *The Elementary School Journal* 73(1), 1–7. In this article, Sid Trubowitz points to the peaks and valleys of energy that characterize a teacher's school year. He poses alternative possibilities regarding the use of time and suggests ways of countering the rigidity of prescribed schedules.

Index

Abstract thinking, 51
Academy of American Poets, 113
Accountability, 17
Across America on an Emigrant Train
    (Murphy), 62–63, 73–74
Active learning, 55, 56, 67–68
Advisory periods, 31
Ames, John, 114
Anderson, Laurie Halse, 62
Anger
  of parents, 78, 81–84, 109
  of teacher, 55, 56, 63, 83, 91, 105,
    109, 110
Annenberg Foundation, 2
Antiviolence programs, 31
Arrow of recitation, 43–44, 58
Atwell, Nancie, 51
Ayers, W., 123

Bank Street College of Education, 76
Bash, Barbara, 97
Bathroom passes, 64
"Better Beginning, A" (Scherer), 126
Black, S., 123
Bomb scare, 52–53, 55
Book talks, 49–50
Boreen, J., 123
Breakfast, standardized tests and,
    90–91, 93
Brock, B. L., 124
Buehl, Doug, 105
Building Parent Partnerships (NEA),
    125

Calkins, Lucy, 51, 113

Calming activities, 31
Caring, 44, 60
Classroom management, 11, 23, 42–43,
    54, 55, 67–69
*Classroom Strategies for Interactive
    Learning* (Buehl), 105
Codell, E. R., 124
Coffee House project, 97–98, 99,
    100–101, 113
Cohen, Saul, 114
Columbine High School, 58, 60
Creative Collaboration (John-Steiner),
    124–125
Critical Friends peer coaching group,
    69–70, 73, 102, 112
Crow, G. M., 124
Crutcher, Chris, 62
Curious George Goes to the Hospital
    (Rey), 40, 49–50
Curtis, Christopher Paul, 95–96

Dahl, Roald, 103
Daniels, Harvey, 37–38, 46, 47
Dante, 114
Darling-Hammond, L., 3
Demonstration lessons, 44–45
Detention policy, 66–67
Disciplined Minds (Gardner), 3
Discussion circles, 43, 57–61. *See also*
    Literature circles
Double-entry journals, 70

Educating Esme (Codell), 124
Educational Horizons, 91–92
Education reform, 40

Eleanor Roosevelt (Freedman), 8–9, 62

Fights, 29–31, 58
Finding One's Way (Crow and
    Matthews), 124
Fishbowling technique, 69–70
Fleishman, Paul, 98
Fletcher, R., 124
Freedman, Russell, 8–9, 62
From First-Year to First-Rate (Brock and
    Grady), 124
Full-class discussion, 57–61
  caring and, 60
  respect and, 58–59
  risk taking and, 58–59

Gallimore, R., 126
Gardner, Howard, 3
Gawandi, A., 124
Giver, The (Lowry), 14, 56, 103–104
Glenn, Mel, 62
Goodnough, A., 2
Grady, M. L., 124

Hawthorne, Nathaniel, 37–38, 39, 46
Hinton, S. E., 62
Homework assignments, 8–9, 24, 78,
    83, 84
House of Seven Gables, The
    (Hawthorne), 37–38, 39, 46
Human Stain, The (Roth), 41

In the Middle (Atwell), 51
I.S. 250. *See* RFK High School/I.S. 250

Johnson, M. K., 123
John-Steiner, Vera, 5, 124–125
Joyful Noise (Fleishman), 98

Kazin, Alfred, 20

Language development, 43
Leadership style, 74–75
"Learning Curve, The" (Gawandi), 124
Learning styles, 42, 110
Libraries, 22, 41, 82, 92, 100

Licensing requirements
  for mentors, 14
  for teachers, 2, 10
Lifeboat for New Teachers, A (Black),
    123
Life experiences, of students, 58–59, 60
Listening, 43–45
  by mentee, 84–85
  by mentor, 23–24
Literature circles, 37–38, 39, 46–48
Literature Circles (Daniels), 37–38, 46
Louis Armstrong Middle School. *See*
    Queens College/Louis Armstrong
    Middle School Collaboration
Lowry, Lois, 14, 56, 103–104
Lunch with the teacher, 30, 60–61

Madeline (Bemelmans), 50
Matthews, L. J., 124
McCourt, Frank, 55–56
Mentee (Maureen)
  anxiety of being observed, 33–35,
    52–53
  bond with mentor, 33–34, 37, 56,
    89–90, 104, 109
  Coffee House project, 97–98, 99,
    100–101, 113
  computer skills of, 111
  and end of mentorship, 102
  and end of school year, 95–96, 102
  exploring school environment, 20–23,
    52
  on full-class discussion, 57–59
  intensity of working one on one,
    42–43
  internship program, 9, 11, 13, 14, 20,
    21–22, 108–109
  job pressures of, 71–72
  list of do's and don'ts for mentees, 119
  list of do's and don'ts for mentors, 117
  literature circles and, 37–38
  mentor selection, 12–14
  most difficult class, 49–53
  moving from theory into practice,
    45–46
  as new teacher, 7–12, 17

observation of mentor, 98–100
outsider status and, 62–65, 73–74
questions of, 23–24, 27–28
reflective log of, 12, 13, 27–28,
    30–31, 33, 53, 88, 104
relating to parents, 8–9, 11, 18, 24,
    29, 77–79, 81–84
school culture and, 62–65, 66–67,
    69–70
search for mentor, 9–12
seeking advice from colleagues, 28–30
on standardized tests, 88–91
teaching voice of, 103–107
vulnerability of, 34–35, 114
Mentoring
checklist for mentors, 115–116
easing licensing requirements and, 2
formal programs, 4
New York City Board of Education
    requirements for, 9–10, 14, 17–18,
    36, 44, 104
New York State requirements, 2, 14
required, 4
by retired teachers, 4, 11, 16
safety needs of mentees, ix
teacher eligibility for, 2
ubiquity of, 15
virtual, 1, 3
as way of training and retaining
    teachers, 1–3
Mentoring Beginning Teachers (Boreen et
    al.), 123
Mentoring New Teachers (Portner), 125
Mentoring (Shea), 126
Mentor (Sid)
checklist for mentors, 115–116
Coffee House project and, 100–101
demonstration lessons and, 44–45
and end of mentorship, 108–114
and end of school year, 96–97, 102,
    108–114
exploring school environment, 20–23,
    39, 43
as former principal, 75–76
on full-class discussion, 59–61
goals as mentor, 16–19, 26

impact of mentoring on, 106–107
involvement in mentorship, 14–16
job pressures of mentee and, 72–73
lesson that fails, 53–56
listening skills and, 43–45
mentors of, 25, 114
as new teacher, 15, 25, 68–69, 85–86
observation of, by mentee, 98–100
on observing teacher, 35–37, 38–41,
    54
questions from mentee, 23–24
reflective log of, 26–27
relating to parents, 79–84
relationship with school principal, 18,
    20, 72
in school community, 100–101
school culture and, 65–66, 67–69
selection as mentor, 11–14
self-talk, 24–27
on standardized tests, 91–94
starts mentorship, 14–16
Merit pay, 89, 110
Murphy, Jim, 62–63, 73–74
Myers, Walter Dean, 62
"My Life With Tests" (Trubowitz),
    89–90, 91–92, 126–127

National Education Association
    (NEA), 125
New Educators Support Team, 2, 102
New York City Board of Education. *See
    also* Queens College/Louis
    Armstrong Middle School
    Collaboration
assignment of teachers, 15
Bulletin on Performance Standards,
    40
licensing requirements, 2, 10, 14
mentoring requirements, 9–10, 14,
    17–18, 36, 44, 104
new-teacher training requirements, 4,
    10
principal mentoring program, 108
principals' examinations, 36
school-based option and, 71–72
New York State

English Language Arts test, 37,
  39–40, 90
mentoring requirements, 2, 14
reading requirements, 78
Niday, D., 123
Notebooks of the Mind (John-Steiner),
  124

Observation
  by buddy teacher, 102, 106
  mentee's reactions to, 33–35, 104–105
  of mentor by mentee, 98–100
  mentor's reactions to, 35–37, 38–41
  by new teachers, 67–69
  by principal/assistant principal, 35,
    69–70, 73–74
"Once Bitten, Twice Shy" (Scott), 126
Open classrooms, 21, 52
Open School Week, 79
Outsiders, The (Hinton), 62
Outsider status, 58–59, 60, 62–65,
  73–74

Padouk, Bertha, 25, 114
Parents
  angry, 78, 81–84, 109
  challenges of, 86
  communicating with, 8–9, 11, 29,
    77–87
  conferences with, 77, 78, 79, 80–81,
    84, 85, 86
  homework and, 8–9, 24, 78, 83, 84
  involvement in class activity, 18, 79,
    80, 86
Parini, J., 125
Peer coaching group, 69–70, 73, 102,
  112
Peer mediation, 31
Portner, H., 125
Potts, J., 123
Preparatory Provisional Teachers
  (PPTs), 14
Principal
  mentor and, 18, 20, 72
  mentoring program for, 108
  observation of teachers, 35, 36,
    69–70, 73–74
  relationship with teachers, 74–76
Professional development. *See also*
  Mentoring
  difficult times in, 54
  lack of, 106
  observation in, 35, 36, 45
  United Federation of Teachers semi-
    nars, 51, 55

Queens College/Louis Armstrong
  Middle School Collaboration
  internship program, 9, 11, 13, 14, 20,
    26–27, 65–66, 68, 86, 99,
    108–109, 112
  museum project, 101

Reading
  book talks and, 49–50
  Coffee House project and, 97–98, 99,
    100–101, 113
  encouraging habit of, 40–41
  libraries and, 22, 41, 82, 92, 100
  literature circles and, 37–38, 39,
    46–48
  reading aloud, 38, 52, 53, 54
  standardized tests and, 92, 94, 106
  technical aspects of, 25
Reading and Writing Workshop, 51
Reflective practice
  of mentee, 12, 13, 27–28, 30–31, 33,
    53, 88, 104
  of mentor, 24–27
Reform, education, 40
Report cards, 86, 95
Respect, 44, 59
Rey, H. A., 49–50
RFK High School/I.S. 250
  collaboration between high school
    and middle school, 22
  Critical Friends peer coaching group,
    69–70, 73, 102, 112
  exploring school environment, 20–23
  nature of students, 20–21
  school culture, 63–70
  service learning and, 20, 61

Risk taking, 58–59
Robins, Maureen, ix–x. *See also* Mentee (Maureen)
Roth, Philip, 41
Rousing Minds to Life (Tharp and Gallimore), 126
Rowley, J. B., 125–126

"Saluting All the King's Mentors" (Parini), 125
Sarason, Seymour, ix–x, 114
Scherer, M., 126
School-based option, 71–72
"School brain," 105
School culture
  new teachers and, 62–65
  rules in, 63–64, 66–67
  wasting time and, 64–65
Schools without walls, 21
School violence, 29–31, 58
Scott, J., 126
Seniority, 2, 71
Service learning, 20, 61
Shea, G. F., 126
Skolnik, Lynn, 4
Small-school initiative, 21
Speak (Anderson), 62
Staff meetings, 66
Standardized tests, 41, 72, 88–94
  breakfast and, 90–91, 93
  effective teaching and, 93
  New York State English Language Arts test, 37, 39–40, 90
  reading and, 92, 94, 106
  strategies for taking, 89, 92–93, 94, 111
Stevenson, Robert Louis, 62–63, 73–74
Student teaching, 2, 9
Summer school, 95
"Supporting New Teachers" (Rowley), 125–126

Teachable moments, 34
Teachers and Writers Collaborative Listserv, 97
Teaching buddies, 102, 106

Teaching style, 23, 44–45, 67–69
Television shows, full-class discussion of, 57–61
Tests. *See* Standardized tests
Tharp, R. G., 126
Theory
  moving into practice from, 45–46
  practice versus, 8–9, 13, 42–43, 45, 46–48
To Become a Teacher (Ayers), 123
To Teach—The Journey of a Teacher (Ayers), 123
Training Mentors Is Not Enough (Portner), 125
Transfers, 71
Troublemakers, 52–53
Trubowitz, Sid, ix–x, 26–27, 126–127. *See also* Mentor (Sid)
"Tyranny of Time, The" (Trubowitz), 127

United Federation of Teachers, 51, 55, 71
U.S. Department of Education, 3
Urban Roosts (Bash), 97

Virtual mentors, 1, 3

Walker in the City, A (Kazin), 20
Walkman listening, 64, 67
Warren, Andrea, 11–12
Watsons Go to Birmingham, The (Curtis), 95–96
What a Writer Needs (Fletcher), 124
Who Killed Mr. Chippendale? (Glenn), 62
"World brain," 105
Writing strategy, 51, 53
Written peer response, 70

About the Authors

Sidney Trubowitz is professor emeritus from Queens College. He has been a high school teacher of English, elementary school teacher, assistant principal and principal of Harlem elementary schools, professor of education, and associate dean and director of the Queens College Center for the Improvement of Education. He is the author of three books and many articles that have appeared in *Phi Delta Kappan, Educational Leadership, Urban Education,* and *The Principal.* His most recent book, *How It Works: Inside a School–College Collaboration,* was coauthored with Paul Longo.

Maureen Picard Robins is a teacher and a writer. She is a staff developer in Queens, New York. Her articles on education and family have appeared in *The Daily News,* msnbc.com, and other journals. She has also created curriculum for the online poetry classroom (www.poets.org) sponsored by the Academy of American Poets and Teachers and Writers Collaborative.